INTERVENTION IN
WORLD POLITICS

Intervention in World Politics

EDITED BY

HEDLEY BULL

CLARENDON PRESS • OXFORD

1984

Oxford University Press, Walton Street, Oxford OX2 6DP
London Glasgow New York Toronto
Delhi Bombay Calcutta Madras Karachi
Kuala Lumpur Singapore Hong Kong Tokyo
Nairobi Dar es Salaam Cape Town
Melbourne Auckland
and associated companies
Beirut Berlin Ibadan Mexico City Nicosia

Oxford is a trade mark of Oxford University Press

Published in the United States
by Oxford University Press, New York

© Oxford University Press 1984

British Library Cataloguing in Publication data
Intervention in world politics.
1. Intervention (International law)
I. Bull, Hedley
341.5'8   JX4481
ISBN 0-19-827467-X

Library of Congress Cataloging in Publication Data
Main entry under title:
Intervention in world politics.
    Based on a series of lectures held at Oxford
University in 1982.
    Includes bibliographical references and index.
    1. Intervention (International law)—Addresses,
essays, lectures.   2. Sovereignty—Addresses, essays,
lectures.   3. International relations—Addresses, essays,
lectures.   4. International law—Addresses, essays,
lectures.   I. Bull, Hedley.
JX4481.I56   1984   341.5'8   83-13368
ISBN 0-19-827467-X

Typeset by Taj Services Ltd., New Delhi
Printed in Hong Kong

Preface

A re-examination of the issue of intervention in world politics is topical for a number of reasons: the progress of Soviet intervention in the Third World; the recovery of belief in military intervention in the United States, so soon after a period of deep disillusion about it; the scepticism evident in Western Europe about this belief; the discovery of a new rationale for intervention—or, more strictly, the rediscovery of an old one—in access to resources, especially oil; the connection that is made between intervention and human rights, and the resurgence of an old belief in humanitarian intervention; the spate of interventionary activity occasioned by movements for national liberation—whether we are thinking of intervention to suppress these movements or to assist them. Intervention is a very central and a very old subject in the study of international relations, and there is a sense in which there is nothing new that can be said about it. But at the same time it is one of those subjects which we have constantly to reassess, in relation to changing circumstances: the underlying questions may be the same, but they keep arising in new forms and being viewed from fresh perspectives.

The following essays, with the exception of my own, were first presented as a course of lectures in the University of Oxford in Hilary Term, 1982, and were made possible by a grant from the Cyril Foster Fund of the University, to whose Board of Management I must express my thanks.

Balliol College   HEDLEY BULL
Oxford

Contents

The Contributors

HEDLEY BULL is Montague Burton Professor of International Relations at Oxford University, and Fellow of Balliol College. He taught previously at the London School of Economics and the Australian National University and is the author of *The Control of the Arms Race* (1961) and *The Anarchical Society. A Study of Order in World Politics* (1977).

STANLEY HOFFMANN is Douglas Dillon Professor of the Civilization of France, and Chairman of the Center for European Studies at Harvard University. His books include *Contemporary Theory in International Relations* (1960), *The State of War* (1965), *Gulliver's Troubles* (1968), *Decline and Renewal: France since the 30s* (1974), *Primacy or World Order?* (1978), *Duties Beyond Borders* (1981), and *Dead Ends* (1983).

ROSALYN HIGGINS is Professor of International Law at the London School of Economics and Member of the Board of Editors of the *American Journal of International Law*. She is the author of *The Development of International Law through the Political Organs of the United Nations* (1963), and *U.N. Peace-Keeping*, vols. I–IV (1969–81).

PHILIP WINDSOR is Reader in International Relations at the London School of Economics and Political Science, and a former staff member of the International Institute for Strategic Studies. His works include *Germany and the Management of Détente* (1971).

DOMINIQUE MOÏSI is Associate Director of the French Institute of International Relations (IFRI) and Associate Professor at the University of Paris X. He is Editor of *Politique Étrangère*.

EDWARD N. LUTTWAK is Senior Fellow at the Georgetown Center for Strategic and International Studies of the Georgetown University in Washington DC, and a professional military adviser. His works include *The Grand Strategy of the Roman Empire* (1976), and *The Grand Strategy of the Soviet Union* (1983).

MICHAEL AKEHURST is Reader in Law at Keele University. He is the author of *The Law Governing Employment in International Organisations* (1967) and *A Modern Introduction to International Law* (fourth edition, 1982).

RICHARD A. FALK is Albert G. Milbank Professor of International Law and Diplomacy at Princeton University. His works include *The Status of Law in International Society* (1970), and *A Study of Future Worlds* (1975).

EVAN LUARD is a former diplomat; delegate to the UN General Assembly, Member of Parliament and junior Minister at the Foreign Office. His many works about international relations include *Conflict and Peace in the Modern International System* (1968), and *The United Nations: How it Works and What it Does* (1978).

I
Introduction
HEDLEY BULL

As a rough guide to what this book is about we may take as our starting-point the kind of definition of intervention offered by the traditional international legal publicists, who (if I may paraphrase them) say that it is dictatorial or coercive interference, by an outside party or parties, in the sphere of jurisdiction of a sovereign state, or more broadly of an independent political community.[1] Intervention in this sense may be forcible or non-forcible (as when it takes the form of economic coercion). It may be direct or indirect (as when a major power uses a minor power as its agent or proxy). It may be open or clandestine (as when the instruments being employed are under the control of secret intelligence agencies). The outside party may be a state or group of states, but on some views also an international organization, a business corporation, or a political party. The jurisdiction that is being interfered with can be a state's jurisdiction over its territory, its citizens, its right to determine its internal affairs or to conduct its external relations. Although some of the authors of the succeeding chapters have departed from this definition in ways that they spell out, they have all had it in mind, and have taken up their positions in relation to it.

A basic condition of any policy that can be called interventionary in this sense is that the intervener should be superior in power to the object of the intervention: it is only because the former is relatively strong and the latter relatively weak that the question arises of a form of interference that is dictatorial or coercive. The great intervening parties of modern history, although by no means the only ones, have been the great powers, and a great power is, among other things, a power that cannot be intervened against: when a once great power becomes the object of foreign intervention, like Turkey in the last century or Russia after 1917, this is a

sign that its status as a great power has lapsed. It is true that
we may find apparent examples of intervention by a smaller
power in the affairs of a stronger, as when Sardinia intervened
in Austria in 1859 alongside Napoleon III, or the New
Zealanders accompanied the Americans into Vietnam, or
lesser members of the Warsaw Pact intervened alongside the
Soviet Union in Czechoslovakia in 1968, but these are
examples of vicarious intervention, the element of dictation
being supplied by the great power ally.

To this we must add that intervention, as I have defined it,
is generally believed to be legally and morally wrong:
sovereign states or independent political communities are
thought to have the right to have their spheres of jurisdiction
respected, and dictatorial interference abridges that right. So
irresistible is this implication that when the rights and wrongs
of policies of intervention are being debated we are inclined to
argue not as to whether or not they are justified, but rather as
to whether or not they constitute intervention.

Of course, intervention in fact is a ubiquitous feature of
modern international relations, perhaps even an inherent
feature of it; moreover, no serious student of the subject can
fail to feel that intervention is sometimes justifiable.[2] Thus it is
widely recognized by international lawyers and moralists that
there are exceptions to the rule of non-intervention. It is often
argued, for example, that intervention is permissible (or is not
intervention) when it is at the invitation of an incumbent
government (an argument used by the Americans in relation
to South Vietnam and the Soviet Union in relation to
Czechoslovakia and Afghanistan); when it takes the form of
counter-intervention, or intervention to assist a state to repel
an intervention which some other party has already begun
(again, an argument commonly invoked by both the superpowers); or when it is undertaken on grounds of self-defence
(the ground on which the Israelis have taken their stand in
justifying their strikes against guerrilla bases in neighbouring
territories, their raid on Entebbe airport in 1976 to release
aircraft hostages, and their bombing in 1981 of the nuclear
installation in Baghdad). It is sometimes contended that
intervention may be justified so as to defend the rights of
foreign subjects of an oppressive ruler (an argument that was

advanced by Grotius himself, that was relied upon in the last century by European powers intervening on behalf of oppressed Christian subjects of the Ottoman Empire, and which some writers, discussed in the chapter by Michael Akehurst, have sought to revive today in relation to the Indian intervention in East Pakistan in 1971, the Vietnamese intervention in Cambodia in 1979, and the Tanzanian intervention to overthrow Amin's rule in the same year in Uganda). Finally, there is much support for the proposition that intervention may be justified when it is collectively authorized by the international community itself through an international organization, general or regional. Christian Wolff, the first writer to state clearly the rule of non-intervention, states it in absolute and uncompromising terms, but he nevertheless holds that it can be overridden by the *civitas maxima*, and today, as Evan Luard notes in his chapter, it is widely held that an intervention is more legitimate if it is not unilateral but has the backing of the United Nations or a regional international organization.

But while it is generally recognized that exceptions must be made to the rule of non-intervention, and the debate concerns the nature and scope of these exceptions, this takes place against the background presumption that intervention in general is wrong. The idea that states have a duty not to engage in intervention is not easily separable from the idea that they have a right to external sovereignty or independence; nor is the idea that states are *equal* in rights, which (in its simplest form, and perhaps also the form in which it is most defensible) means no more than that they are all equally or alike sovereign—whether a state is large or small, socialist or non-socialist, European or non-European, is thought to have no bearing on its rights of independence. Today, these ideas of the equal rights of states to have their sovereignty respected, and their corresponding duty to refrain from dictatorial interference within one another's recognized spheres of jurisdiction, are proclaimed in more extravagant terms than ever before. The Third World states in the post-1945 era, like the Latin American states in the last century and early in this century, conscious that their sovereignty is compromised by constant and endemic intervention, cling to the rhetoric of sovereignty as one of the means available to them of defending it.

It is important to remember, however, that these ideas were virtually unknown, at least in their modern legal form, in what we may call the international political experience of Asia, Africa, and the Americas before the incorporation of the latter within the expanding European states system. Not only are they not part of the indigenous diplomatic traditions of any continent other than Europe, they are only recent ideas in the history of Europe itself: it was only in the mid-eighteenth century, at the hands of Wolff and Vattel, that the doctrines of the equal rights of states to sovereignty, and of their duty of non-intervention, were first clearly stated. Since that time, moreover, their impact even within Europe has been limited—on the one hand by the ancient hierarchies of status and precedent among European monarchies and republics, curtailed but not eliminated by the Congress of Vienna in 1815, and on the other hand by the new hierarchy of rights determined by power, that gave rise to the especially modern idea of the rights and duties peculiar to the status of a great power, still embodied in the privileges of permanent members of the United Nations Security Council. To this there was added, from the time of the Hague Peace Conferences of 1899 and 1907, and reinforced with the founding of the League of Nations, a growing feeling that the ideas of sovereignty, equality, and non-intervention were an obstacle to the progressive development of international organization. Even by the time of the Second World War these ideas were far from having been fully realized even within the European or Western world (the white nations of the British Commonwealth, for example, were preoccupied with the pursuit of equal status throughout the inter-war period), quite apart from their lack of effective application to the non-European or non-Western world, and indeed during the Second World War they were wholly repudiated in their application to the European continent itself by the hierarchical system of Hitler's New Order.

Today, it would seem, at least at first sight, that the rule of non-intervention and the rule of mutual respect for sovereign jurisdiction, of which it is part, are remote from the facts of international life. On the one hand, under the influence of Third World majorities in the political organs of the United Nations, legal prohibitions of intervention have multiplied; on the other hand, interventionary activity of one kind or another is so widespread that it is sometimes said to be endemic or 'structural' in nature.

The essays that follow do not provide a fully comprehensive account of this state of affairs but they do enquire into some of its most essential features. How does interventionary activity at the present time relate to the particular character of the international political system and its prevailing rules? What does international law have to say about the way the distinction can at present be drawn between legitimate and illegitimate interference or intrusion? What determines the interventionary behaviour of the two superpowers, is their intervention 'structural' in character, and is it correct or incorrect to treat the United States and the Soviet Union as if they were similar or comparable in respect of their interventionary behaviour? Is there a right of intervention to secure access to vital natural resources, and if there is, can it be prudent to exercise it? What accounts for the apparent success of France as an interventionist power in post-colonial Africa, and how far in fact has France been successful? What is the relationship between intervention and the processes of national liberation—what can be said about the determinants, the incidence, and the legitimacy on the one hand of intervention to suppress national liberation, and on the other hand of intervention to promote it? How does the emerging law of non-intervention relate to the emerging law of human rights, and is there today, as is sometimes alleged, a right of 'humanitarian intervention'? What is the pattern of interventionary activity in the weak and vulnerable states of the Third World, and have the latter become more or less able to resist it? What has been our experience of intervention that is sanctioned collectively by the UN or some other international organization, and what is the promise of proposals to substitute, for the old rule prohibiting intervention, a new rule requiring that it must be collectively authorized?

Underlying these piecemeal enquiries there are three basic questions, to which I shall return in the concluding chapter.

First, what is the place of intervention in contemporary world politics—who are the interveners, what are the prevailing forms or modes of intervention, how endemic can intervention be said to have become? Secondly, is the gap between the rule of non-intervention and the facts of intervention now so vast that the former has become a mockery with which it would be better to dispense altogether, or does the proscription of intervention remain a vital part of the normative structure on which international order depends? Thirdly, if the rule of non-intervention does indeed remain essential to world order at the present time, how should it be formulated, modified, or adapted, to take account of the circumstances of our own times?

NOTES

1   Cf. L. Oppenheim: *International Law*, vol. I, Longmans, London, 1905.

2   The best general account of the rule of non-intervention is John Vincent's *Non-Intervention and International Order*, Princeton University Press, Princeton, NJ, 1974.

2

The Problem of Intervention

STANLEY HOFFMANN

A general presentation on the subject of intervention is likely to contain little that is original, and to consist only of an endless series of classifications. The reason for this is very simple. The subject is practically the same as that of international politics in general from the beginning of time to the present. This makes it, of course, both important and very topical. If one looks only at the events of 1981–2, one finds the following: perhaps not a resurgence of American military interventionism (neither the American administration nor the American people are ready for new Vietnams and a distinction must be made between the administration's rhetoric and reality), but some new American military activities in El Salvador, together with threats concerning Nicaragua; Cuban support for resistance movements in El Salvador and in Guatemala; the Soviet Union's continuing operations and difficulties in Afghanistan; a military coup in Poland, with which the Soviet Union clearly had something to do (the imposition of martial law followed a whole series of Soviet threats over several months); the fading of French military activities in Chad, replaced by Libyan ones in Chad and in Sudan; a continuing contest on the battlefield and in the United Nations over who constitutes the legitimate government of Cambodia; an attempt by the United States government to revoke the Clark amendment prohibiting American intervention in the civil strife in Angola, and the visit of Mr Savimbi to Washington; continuing negotiations by the group of five on the future of Namibia; an Israeli invasion of Lebanon aimed at changing the political structure as well as the military balance there. All these events clearly come under the heading of intervention: they occur on every continent, involving every kind of act and every kind of actor.

I shall start with a discussion of intervention as a set of facts, so as to present a broad picture of intervention in international relations. Then I shall look at it as an issue, as a problem to be solved, before coming to the obvious conclusion that it is insoluble.

I.   *Intervention as a set of facts*

Let us begin with a definition. Nothing can be more static or less rewarding. Nevertheless, when one talks about concepts such as aggression, or imperialism, or intervention, a definition is necessary. We do have to distinguish intervention from other forms of international politics. In the widest sense, to be sure, every act of a state constitutes intervention. When the Israelis, in 1981, bombed the nuclear reactor near Baghdad, it clearly was a rather brutal form of intervention. In India, where perceptions of the outside world sometimes almost reduce it to one single country, Pakistan, the recent American decision to sell F-16 aeroplanes to Pakistan is being seen as an intervention in Indian affairs, just as in Algeria the American decision to sell arms to Morocco is seen as an intervention in North African affairs. Many Americans thought that the French–Mexican communiqué of 1981 about El Salvador constituted an intervention; they certainly believe that the French decision to sell arms to Nicaragua is an intervention, and if one listens to Radio Moscow, which competes for the domination of the short waves with the BBC World Service, one hears day after day that the NATO powers are blatantly intervening in the internal affairs of Poland and blocking its process of renewal. So clearly anything can constitute an intervention; indeed, even non-acts can constitute interventions: remember the effects of British and French non-intervention in the Spanish Civil War. It was Talleyrand, the great cynic and wise man, who said that intervention and non-intervention are the same thing. The West German decision not to take sanctions against the Soviet Union over Poland does, in a sense, constitute an intervention on the side of General Jaruzelski, if not of Mr Brezhnev, and if one talks to Palestinians, one will certainly hear that America's indifference toward the autonomy talks and the Camp David process, and America's failure to protest against the use of American-made weapons in the invasion of Lebanon by Israel amount to intervention on the side of the Israelis.

For clarity's sake, however, ways must be found of delimiting the subject. The literature provides three ways of doing it. One is by reference to the type of activity involved: a classic definition by Oppenheim restricts interventions to those acts which constitute 'dictatorial interference'. My own preference is not to define intervention by reference to the type of activity. To say that only acts of dictatorial interference constitute interventions narrows the subject too much. After all, the purpose of intervention is the same as that of all other forms of foreign policy; it is to make you do what I want you to do, whether or not you wish to do it. But how I try to achieve this can take an enormous variety of forms. Some are explicitly coercive interventions, through the use or threat of force—from sending an army into your country if you don't behave to unleashing terrorists such as the assassination squads of President Qaddafi. Another kind of explicitly coercive intervention takes the form of economic coercion—trade and credit sanctions, boycotts, embargoes. Explicit coercion can also be achieved through subsidies, aid to revolutionary groups or to opponents of a regime that one wants to unseat. Other kinds of intervention I call implicitly coercive. These do not constitute obvious dictatorial interference, and yet they are still interventions aimed at forcing you to do something which you might otherwise not particularly want to do. One form this takes—a very old one in international politics—is bribery: rewards to friends, encouraging them to do things which they may have some misgivings about, but for which they can then be recompensed. One modern form of bribery is aid to shaky governments designed to make them both less shaky and more favourable to one's own side. If a state is very wealthy, it can resort to bribery on a large scale; the United States has practised this, sometimes with virtuosity, sometimes with mixed results (I am thinking of American support of the Shah of Iran, and of present American policies in Pakistan). But aiding shaky governments so that they do what one wants is also what the Soviet Union and the Cubans have been attempting in places like Angola and Ethiopia. In the protracted Lebanese civil war, Israeli support of Major Haddad in Southern Lebanon has been one way for Israel to exert influence. Another form of intervention which is implicitly coercive but not obviously dictatorial, is propaganda bombardment, so to speak. This bewildering variety of techniques explains why, in my opinion, one cannot delimit intervention by reference to the type of activity; the choice of the latter depends on the specific objective, on the circumstances, on the intervening state's resources, and on the kinds of policy instruments at its disposal.

A second means of delimitation is by reference to the type of actor. The word has been used so loosely that one sometimes talks about intervention by private groups. I prefer to limit consideration of it to acts of states, of groups fighting for statehood, and of collections of states, such as international organizations. In other words, I include as examples of intervention the activities of private organizations, like multinational corporations, for instance, only if they are backed by a state, or act on behalf of a state (multinational corporations, incidentally, are not the only such actors; there was a period in the beginning of the cold war when American labour unions exerted considerable influence in various other parts of the world, in Western Europe and in Africa, for instance, setting up friendly labour unions; this was not totally independent of the policies of the US government).

The most important delimitation is the third: by type of target. Here, I propose to restrict the concept of intervention to *acts which try to affect not the external activities, but the domestic affairs of a state*. In other words, I would not consider as an intervention, for the present purposes, acts such as the quasi-annexation of the Golan Heights by Israel or, to take a very different example, the German declaration of unlimited submarine warfare in the First World War. I will not, in other words, look at intervention as an act, or a series of acts, aimed at the foreign relations or the external behaviour of a state. I restrict it to acts aimed at affecting the domestic affairs of the state, either because the state itself is the target of attempts at control from the outside (this is particularly the case when the nature of authority in that state is in question, when it is not clear who should be or who is the legitimate authority in civil wars for instance), or because an attempt at affecting domestic affairs is deemed the best way of influencing the external behaviour of a state (if one wants an actor to behave in a certain way on the world stage, what better method is there than to see to it that it has the 'right' kind of government?).

Even when one has restricted the subject to acts aimed at affecting the domestic affairs of others, one still finds that it is ubiquitous. It is therefore necessary to introduce some more dynamic considerations.

There are, in international affairs, some fundamental contradictions which underlie the whole subject of intervention. The most fundamental is this. International society, for some centuries now, has been founded on the principle of sovereignty; in other words, the state is supposed to be the master of what goes on inside its territory, and international relations are relations between sovereign states, each one of which has certain rights and obligations derived from the very fact of statehood. If one accepts the principle of sovereignty as the corner-stone of international society, this means (and it has been recognized by international lawyers ever since the time of Wolff and Vattel in the eighteenth century) that intervention, defined as an act aimed at influencing the domestic affairs of a state, is quite clearly illegitimate. On the other hand, the principle of sovereignty also entails the rule of self-help, and there is an innate contradiction between the illegitimacy of intervention and the legitimacy of self-help. In fact, the choice in international affairs has never been between intervening and observing the sacred principle of non-intervention. The choice has always been between individual intervention and collective intervention, or else between the establishment of conditions in which intervention will become less likely, and living in conditions in which intervention is more likely. In other words, the key variable is the nature of the international system. This first, most basic contradiction results from the very nature of an international milieu of decentralized units with no common superior.

There is a second contradiction which issues from the particular nature of international society in the twentieth century. The principle of sovereignty is not the only corner-stone of contemporary international relations; the constitutive principle of international order in this century is not the respect of *any* sovereignty, but the principle of self-determination—a principle of both domestic and external legitimacy. We profess to believe, rightly or wrongly, that precisely because the notion of sovereignty, which leads to self-help, can become a source of chaos, chaos would be best avoided if all the states were based on the principle of self-determination or of nationality. This adds an entirely new element to the study of intervention, because it seems to legitimize intervention on behalf of self-determination and raises the whole issue of national liberation movements and of their status in the world.

There is a third contradiction. One finds recurring in international affairs a belief that the best way of ensuring some kind of order or moderation, the best way of preventing state sovereignty and even the principle of national self-determination from leading to chaos, the best way of starving out opportunities for intervention, is to insist on a principle of governmental legitimacy. This is the familiar idea, according to which the best possible conditions for order in international affairs will exist if all the governments are of a certain type. Such a notion lay behind the Holy Alliance of 1815, with its commitment to dynastic legitimacy. To take another example, many liberals in the nineteenth century believed that (as Kant maintained) the best kind of international order would be one in which all governments were constitutional governments. Such notions introduce another paradox, because they seem to legitimize intervention to promote a principle of governmental legitimacy.

If one looks at the historical evolution of intervention, there are two questions, the answers to which determine its shape and the scope. First, is there at any given moment a prevailing principle of domestic legitimacy or not? Those familiar with Raymond Aron's book on *Peace and War* will remember that he sees in this particular question the criterion that determines whether an international system is 'homogeneous' or 'heterogeneous'.[1] An international system is homogeneous when all the units have the same principle of domestic legitimacy. In such a situation this does not mean that there will be no interventions; in the seventeenth and eighteenth centuries, when there was a dominant principle of domestic legitimacy, and most of the units were monarchies, many wars nevertheless took place because of contending claims to the same throne. Much international politics consisted of seeing to it that state A, or rather king A, placed (or was forcibly prevented from placing) a brother-in-law, a cousin, the wife of a cousin, or the wife of a brother-in-law, on a foreign throne. In other words, manipulation of the dynastic principle was a way of ensuring alliances and of expanding influence; this persisted even into the nineteenth century. It was the cause or the pretext for the Franco-Prussian War of 1870–1, when the French Emperor thought it highly insulting and dangerous to have a Hohenzollern as a potential King of Spain. What produces interventions even when there exists a single principle of domestic legitimacy is the perennial dialectic of relations between the weak and the strong.

When there are several principles of domestic legitimacy in competition—that is to say when, to use Aron's definition, the international system is heterogeneous—the gravest danger exists for international order. The best example here is that of the French Revolution, where a violent clash occurred between the old dynastic principle, upheld by the main courts in Europe, and the new French principle, enshrined in the Declaration of 15 December 1792, which essentially proclaimed French support for what we would now call movements of national liberation in various countries. The result was a kind of war of religion between the two principles, a war which was confusing when the principle of national liberation came to be upheld by Napoleon. As is usual in international affairs, the clash of principles became a clash of power, and French expansionism took precedence over French revolutionary Messianism; what had been supposed to be a support for national liberation became a pretext for territorial annexation.

If one moves on a little in time, one comes to the classical scene of 1815, discussed in Henry Kissinger's *A World Restored*.[2] At the Congress of Vienna and in the world outside, the conflict was between three different principles: the monarchic or dynastic principle upheld by the Austrians and by the Russians, representative government favoured by the British and the French, and a more democratic and national principle supported by the liberal and nationalist forces operating in several countries. In Vienna, as is well known, there was a solemn debate between Metternich and the Tsar, who were advocating intervention on behalf of the dynastic principle, and the British, Castlereagh and later Canning, who essentially rejected the idea of intervention.

Another era in which interventions proliferate because there is no agreement on the principle of domestic legitimacy, is the period between the two World Wars, when three conflicting principles were again battling with each other: the democratic one, which seemed to have been enshrined in the Versailles Treaty and in the League of Nations Covenant, what could be called the Fascist principle, and the Communist one. The best example of the resulting chaos, the crucible really, was the Spanish Civil War, in which all three forces were at work, two in the form of outright intervention and one in the form of a shabby non-intervention.

Still, nothing may ever have been quite as complex as the situation which prevails now, in the period since the end of the Second World War. The following elements of the international system make for universal intervention. First, there are all the battles over the application of the principle of self-determination. Everybody pays lip-service to it as the constitutive principle of international order, and yet it is fraught with so many uncertainties that it is a major source of strife and a major invitation to external intrusions. In much of the world, a conflict rages between the principle of self-determination, which assumes that the state should be the expression of a nation, and the existence of borders which have very often been artificially carved up by the colonial powers. Is the principle of self-determination an essentially theoretical notion, under whose influence independence is given to states within those artificial borders, and a kind of licence granted to these states to try to make a nation out of the people within them, or must it be taken so seriously that one has to concede to every group which considers itself a nation the right to set itself up as a state, even at the expense of the traditional borders and of pre-existing states? The longest list of interventions is of those that have occurred over and around the uncertainties of the principle of self-determination. In no particular order, either geographic or chronological, one can mention the international debate over

Taiwan, and over the independence of South Vietnam, the wars between Somalia and Ethiopia, and between Ethiopia and Eritrea, the attempted secession of Biafra from Nigeria, the secession of Bangladesh from Pakistan, the Chinese claim to Tibet, the Indonesian claim to West Irian and East Timor, the recent battles over Western Sahara, Syrian and Israeli interventions in Lebanon, resulting from the clash of two nationalities—Israeli and Palestinian—over the same area, the Turkish interventions in Cyprus, Black African support for independence movements in Zimbabwe and Namibia: there has been a maelstrom of interventions around the mists of self-determination.

A second contemporary factor is the conflict between two versions of what constitutes democratic self-government. Everybody, again, pays lip-service to one principle of governmental legitimacy, which is the democratic principle; but we have in fact two different principles in competition, the Western notion of democracy—which, to simplify, I shall call democracy—and the communist version of democracy—which, to simplify, I shall call totalitarianism. What happened in late 1981 and early1982 in Poland is a very good example of that particular contest. To the West, the fact that the Polish workers had their own idea about domestic legitimacy was a triumph for democracy; for the Soviet Union, it was a challenge to their particular version of party control. Soviet intervention in Afghanistan must also be mentioned in this context—as well as the attempted American invasion of Cuba in 1961, or the successful American intervention in Guatemala in 1954.

But these are not the only focal points for intervention. The world would be too simple if only these existed. We find, in addition, a number of other factors, which are very hard to fit into any neat theoretical scheme. There are, for instance, some interventions which could be described as belatedly colonial, such as Argentina's attempt at seizing control of the Falkland Islands on the basis of dubious and distant historical claims, and others which could be called colonial left-overs. When General de Gaulle, in his inimitable way, decolonized, he did it by signing treaties with a number of African states, which allowed France to intervene in the domestic affairs of

those states whenever the Government felt sufficiently
threatened to call on France to come to its help; and those
treaties were acted upon quite a number of times. We have
witnessed a new fuel of interventions in recent years: the force
of Islamic fundamentalism, which President Qaddafi and
Ayatollah Khomeini claim to incarnate. Libya has tried to
overthrow or to control several governments, and the war
between Iraq and Iran is concerned not only with territorial
claims but with each side's attempt to overthrow the other's
ruler. Finally, there are splits in the communist world, rival
versions of the totalitarian orthodoxy, and the conflict over
Cambodia—whether the legitimate government of Cambodia
is either a government of murderers who happen to be real
Cambodians, or a government of puppets who happen to be
put in by the Vietnamese—is largely a consequence of that
split. In other words, a generalization of intervention is of the
essence of the highly heterogeneous post-war international
system, and it is aggravated by a second question.

The first question referred to the presence or absence, at any
given moment, of a principle of domestic legitimacy. It dealt,
so to speak, with the frame and foundations of the house of
international relations. The second question deals with what
goes on within the house: is there a mechanism of international order and moderation at a given moment or not? The only
mechanism of moderation known in the past, alas, has been
the balance-of-power system, and we must briefly examine the
relations between intervention and the balance of power. It is
a very complicated relationship, because, on the one hand,
when the balance-of-power system functions well, it deters, or
coerces, trouble-makers, and therefore either limits the
opportunities for interventions which trouble-makers may
want to exploit, or at least deprives these of some of the results
they expect from their intervention. In other words, when the
system works it has the effect of protecting the independence of
the weakest states from the designs of a particular trouble-
maker; and if one looks at the history of recurrent Russian
meddling in the affairs of the decomposing Ottoman Empire,
in the eighteenth and nineteenth centuries, one sees that very
often Russian advances were stopped or limited by the
operation of the balance of power, as in the Crimean War of

1854–6. or in the big Eastern crisis of 1875–8. Also, the fact that the balance-of-power system is a mechanism of shifting alliances means that in order to operate well it has to be quite indifferent to domestic regimes: against a trouble-maker, you ought to be able to align yourself with any other sort of state, whether its government is of the left or right, whether it is monarchical or representative; this requirement for flexibility, which entails a certain indifference to the domestic order, explains why, for instance, British Foreign Ministers were opposed to Austrian intervention in Spain in the 1820s.

However, this is only part of the story. When the balance of power operates, it dampens interventions, but it certainly does not stop them, for a whole variety of reasons. The first one is that the balancing mechanism itself, when it functions, opens up possibilities of collective intervention. The best way of my preventing you from intervening and reaping benefits for yourself alone, is by our intervening all together, so that we can each gain a little bit. And that, of course, is not good for the target of the intervention. But this was very often what happened in the age of the European Concert; this is the way in which the Greek crisis of the 1820s and the independence of Belgium in 1830 were handled; this is the way in which the French were prevented from being the only beneficiaries of the big crisis in Lebanon in 1860–1. Again, in order to prevent the Russians from gaining inch after inch at the expense of the Ottoman Empire, the European powers resorted recurrently to collective interventions: in the finances of the Ottoman Empire, which were being put under collective supervision, over the establishment of an autonomous Crete, over the independence of Albania, and so on. In other words, for a small power the balance of power could be a mixed blessing because instead of being eaten by one great power, one could be gnawed by all five or six.

Secondly, the balancing mechanism opened up not merely the possibility of collective intervention, but also the possibility of the great powers simply getting together, quite cynically, to carve up the target. The most extreme case is that of unfortunate Poland, which nature put in a position where no people should be: between the Germans and the Russians. But in fact Poland, which one always gives as an example, is only one instance among many, for there were several successive partitions of the Ottoman Empire, decided collectively by the European powers, giving rise to the emergence of feuding Balkan successor states.

Thirdly, interventions continued quite simply because from time to time the balance of power did not work; the mechanism of alignments against the trouble-maker did not always operate. This is how the Austrians annexed Bosnia in 1908; this is how the British came to occupy Egypt, and then spent sixty years explaining that they wanted to give up; this is how Napoleon III got involved in Italy in the 1850s, at a time when no power was willing to stop him; this is how Bismarck began his march to the unification of Germany.

A fourth reason why intervention was perfectly compatible with the balance of power was that the very indifference of the balance toward domestic regimes made it perfectly possible at times for one particular country to intervene in the domestic affairs of a state without being stopped by others. The indifference of the system as such cut both ways. It meant, on the one hand, that there would be no collective interventions to impose, let us say, the monarchic or the constitutional principle, but it also meant that when the Russians came in to help the Austrians crush revolutions in Austria or in Hungary, and when Russians again intervened to crush revolutions in Poland, nobody did anything about it.

And finally interventions flourished because the balance-of-power system was never applied overseas—to affairs outside the European system; if one looks at the way in which most colonial empires were established in the nineteenth century, it was through intervention and the manipulation of local forces.

So, the balance-of-power system was unsatisfactory for purposes of controlling intervention. Of course, when there is no balance-of-power system and the world lives under a bipolar system, things are more unsatisfactory still, and this has been the experience, not only at the time of Thucydides, who gives an account of interventions in a system dominated by Sparta and Athens, but again in the international system that followed the Second World War. In the periods of acute cold war—in other words, the late forties, fifties, and early sixties, and again in the late seventies and the eighties—the forms of intervention caused by the rivalry between the United States and the Soviet Union become countless. There are interventions for self-protection, for protecting one's stakes, for protecting one's clients: in mild form, for instance, the American intervention in the 1948 election campaign in Italy; or the American landing of marines on the sunny beaches of Lebanon in the midst of all the swimmers in 1958; the American intervention in South Vietnam, much less mild; the recurrent Soviet interventions in Eastern Europe. These self-protecting interventions are best summarized by the so-called Brezhnev Doctrine of 1968—fraternal assistance to socialism—and by what some authors have called the Johnson doctrine of the 1960s, the declaration that the United States would not tolerate the threat of communism in the Latin American or Central American sphere (although actually it antedates Johnson and can be traced back to the Rio treaty). Self-protection is also the motive of the recurrent American policy of throwing a mantle of protection over regimes, to safeguard them against internal upheaval when they happen to sit on very large amounts of natural resources to which the West wants access—as in the Middle East. But self-protection is only one form. Some interventions are sanctions—several American measures after the Soviet invasion of Afghanistan and the proclamation of martial law in Poland for instance. There are also counter-offensive interventions—the US intervention in Guatemala in 1954; the attempt at the Bay of Pigs. There are interventions for the expansion of influence—the Soviet Union in Afghanistan, the Soviet Union and Cuba in Angola and Ethiopia, Vietnam in Cambodia.

Why do we find this generalization of intervention in the current bipolar international system? It is partly because there is an ideological contest—two ways of life, two conceptions of both domestic and international order in conflict. Another reason is the abundance of targets of opportunity: the world now consists of many artificial states which are states only by general tolerance, but which are wracked by enormous internal difficulties—weak regimes, ethnic conflicts, religious or communal tensions, economic turmoil—and therefore constitute easy prey for the super-powers. A further reason is the phenomenon of compensation, what some authors have called the internalization of conflict; since the major stakes in international affairs are somewhat unreachable because of the fear of nuclear war (the major stakes are still in Europe and in the Far East, but neither side can do much about them without risk of blowing up the world), by compensation it is easier to fight over what government will be in control of what territory in areas which are less explosive. The moderation of means induced by the peril of nuclear war, and the superpowers' need to limit their goals for the same reason, leave ample room for interventions aimed at changing the international milieu by affecting the domestic political make-up of other countries.

Such is the scope of the phenomenon, and the reasons for it. One last word about its prevalence in the bipolar competition. The best example here is provided by Kissinger's foreign policy. His own ideal was a return to moderation, to a world in which there would be a clear distinction between domestic and external affairs, in which foreign policy would concern itself only with the external activities of states, whatever their domestic regimes; that explains why, as a good *Realpolitiker*, he was perfectly willing to deal with a communist state like China or even with a radical one like Assad's Syria. On the other hand, the very logic of the bipolar conflict obliged him to behave much more like Metternich than like Castlereagh. Since he was in effect obsessed with the Soviet–American conflict, one of his constant concerns was to see to it that countries in what he considered to be the preserve of the West did not acquire regimes hostile to it. This fear was carried to its most extreme length in his policy towards Allende's Chile. The very logic of the system—of the bipolar conflict—led him to a series of interventions in domestic affairs, beyond the pale of inter-state relations.

II.　*Intervention as an issue*

If such is the scope of the problem, the question may be asked: what can one do about it? I now come to the treatment of intervention as a problem to be solved.

There have been two kinds of attempts at controlling intervention. Both have failed. The first is that of international law and the United Nations Charter. The Charter, interestingly enough, is not a very satisfactory instrument when it comes to the problem of intervention, because it deals with it in a very limited way. It concerns itself first of all only with certain types of actions. What it bans is the use of force and the threat of force. As I noted earlier, there are many other ways of intervening, in which force, or even the threat of force remain implicit, below the visible surface. Furthermore, the Charter only aims at protecting the territorial integrity and the political independence of a state; it does not deal with other ways of undermining a state, such as trying to change the nature of its government. One could argue for instance that what has been happening in Warsaw does not affect the territorial integrity of Poland. As for its political independence, that in a sense has been given away since 1945, and is not at stake. What is at stake is something quite different: the autonomy of the government itself. And indeed, the United Nations Charter is very silent on what has been the most frequent type of intervention, intervention to determine the outcome of a civil war—whether we think about South Vietnam, or Lebanon, or Chad, or Angola, or Afghanistan. The Charter is based on a model which draws a sharp distinction between external and domestic affairs; the evil against which it is supposed to operate is that of the massive crossing of established borders by armies; and that has not been the main problem of post-war international relations. It does not really deal with such cases as Poland in 1981 or, say, a state buying friends with arms, when those friends are fairly shaky regimes.

The second attempt at controlling intervention has been the attempt by international or regional organizations, or by what some of my colleagues would call international regimes, at introducing a modicum of order, by collectivizing intervention in the way in which the European Concert sometimes collectivized it. If one looks at the record, one can reach three conclusions about it. The first one is that in the political domain—in political conflicts—collectivization has been of very limited effectiveness. The most extensive attempt, horridly complicated, was the intervention by the United Nations in the Congo crisis of 1960; it led to an endless series of knots into which the members of the UN tied themselves, over who the legitimate government in the Congo was and what the new nation's proper borders were. The most recent attempts at collectivizing have been through the Organization of African Unity. They have not worked very well in Chad, nor in relation to Amin's Uganda. Nor has the UN been able to save Lebanon from further, brutal outside interventions. The most persistent attempt has been collective pressure on South Africa through the UN, including the use of sanctions; results have been very meagre. The only successful attempt at an intervention on behalf of the international community that one can readily summon to mind, was not really a collective attempt at all—it was the skilful diplomacy of Lord Soames in the case of Zimbabwe, the exception which does not quite confirm the rule.

Secondly, interestingly enough, collective intervention has become routine in economic affairs. While most states resent attempts by other states to intervene through the use of economic instruments, the resort to such tools of intervention by bodies like the International Monetary Fund, the World Bank, or the OECD has become perfectly normal. All IMF loans come with conditions relating to the balance of payments policies, or the monetary and budgetary policies of the recipients; these are forms of intervention; they are collective and they are not only accepted, they are sometimes even welcomed.

The third conclusion concerns a failure, again; the attempt by the Carter administration at establishing a collective regime of intervention in order to stop or slow down nuclear proliferation, and to go beyond the strictures of the 1968 non-proliferation treaty and the rather weak safeguards of the International Atomic Energy Agency. Here, we were back in the political sphere. This effort failed because of disagreements about what would constitute the most effective form of intervention—the debate between those who thought that denial was best and those who thought that controls were best; and it failed above all because of the conflict between the logic of world order, which tried to impose a collective and restrictive regime impartially on all possible proliferaters, and the logic of the cold war, which suggested that one be kind to those potential proliferaters who are one's friends in the cold war. The issue over which this came to a boil is that of Pakistan's nuclear programme. The record of control of interventions in international law and organization is bleak; what still prevails is self-help, as was demonstrated by the Israeli raid against Iraq's reactor—called by some, grimly or jokingly, the most effective anti-proliferation measure so far.

I now turn to the theory or philosophy of the subject. If one cannot control intervention, one can at least speculate; indeed, there is at present a very big debate on the legitimacy of intervention. If interventions, like wars, are here to stay, perhaps all one can do is pontificate. This allows one, if not to stop them, at least to judge them. Thus, I shall now examine attempts by theorists to write guidelines distinguishing between what is legitimate intervention and what is not.

Here, liberals find themselves with a special problem. For a Marxist-Leninist, there is no problem in making a double-edged use of international law; the principle of sovereignty is there to defend one's conquests, and one is justified in intervening to protect them. On the other hand, one can provide legitimate aid to liberation movements, aimed at changing the correlation of forces, at exploiting and pushing forward those deep forces of history which justify carrying the revolution further. For a liberal, however, there is a dilemma. On the one hand, liberalism is a universalistic conception: it assumes that there are values which transcend the mere fact of sovereignty, or the mere legal rights entailed by sovereignty; it holds that we have the moral right to judge what goes on inside the sovereign unit, and that there are some ethical principles and human rights which transcend borders. So, from this viewpoint, liberalism contains a logic of rightful intervention. On the other hand, liberals also recognize that violence and war are the greatest enemies of liberty, and would be the inevitable result of generalized intervention; that is a pragmatic argument against it. And there is also a moral argument against intervention, which was made particularly strongly by John Stuart Mill: liberty can really only come from oneself. You cannot receive it from the outside. This explains why Kant is so silent on the issue of intervention. For Kant, the pre-conditions of world peace were essentially what we call today self-determination and self-government. Nowhere does he advocate a crusade to establish self-determination and self-government, but nowhere does he proscribe it either. This also accounts for the contradictions of Woodrow Wilson, who had a splendid vision of a harmonious world reshaped according to the Fourteen Points, yet did not want to accept too tough a series of principles and obligations of enforcement in the Covenant of the League of Nations. He wanted (and in a sense fell over) article 10, but was dubious about actual collective security.

What one finds at present in the literature is agreement on two issues and disagreement on three. The two issues on which there seems to be agreement are the following. First, humanitarian intervention is deemed legitimate: intervention by force against a state which practises genocide on a large scale or which would, for instance, starve its inhabitants. This is the argument that was used by some to justify the removal of such monsters as Idi Amin and Bokassa, to explain Indian intervention for the independence of Bangladesh, and to defend the elimination of Pol Pot by invasion. The problem with this argument is that in the real world things are more ambiguous; it is hard to know whether an intervention which starts as a humanitarian move does not later become self-serving. The case of Cambodia is pertinent: Vietnam's attack started as a successful attempt at removing Pol Pot, but ended as the imposition of Vietnamese rule. Since international mechanisms have been paralysed—since there are really no cases in which international organization has given a collective sanction to this sort of humanitarian intervention—it has always been done by self-help. It was Tanzania that went into Uganda, not the Organization of African Unity, which was divided over the issue. So that even in this one instance in which all the theorists agree, there is a need to inject a loud note of practical caution.

I would say the same about the second issue on which theorists, for the most part, agree: that interventions to promote the principle of self-determination are legitimate. (An exception is Charles Beitz, who denies moral validity to the principle.) Michael Walzer, in his admirable book on *Just and Unjust Wars*, and in a subsequent article in which he replies to his critics, states that interventions to support the

Hungarian insurrection aimed at secession from Austria in 1848, or to help the Blacks obtain a state of their own in contemporary South Africa, would have been or would be legitimate.[3] But, here again, there are great practical difficulties. First, there is no agreement on the nature and size of the unit that can legitimately claim self-determination: a major issue, as the Biafran civil war showed. Secondly, what happens when two nations fight over the same ground, as in Palestine? Thirdly, even if one firmly believes in the moral importance of securing the principle of self-determination and even when the borders are fairly clear, there may often be several contenders to be the rightful beneficiaries of the principle: in the case of Zimbabwe, for example, Bishop Muzorewa, Nkomo, and Mugabe. In other words, even here, in practice, the need for prudence overwhelms, in my opinion at least, the moral argument for intervention.

Now come the cases of disagreement among theorists. The first is the case of counter-intervention. Walzer argues that if state A has intervened in a civil war on one side, state B is entitled to intervene on the other side in order to restore a certain kind of balance. It is a neutral rule, like most rules of international law. There has been a debate over this, some people saying that intervention is only legitimate on the side of the 'good guys', so that if the first side that intervenes is on the good side, no counter-intervention aimed merely at restoring an artificial balance ought to be allowed. My own position is that, in the abstract, counter-intervention is indeed legitimate only when intervention occurred on the side of anti-democratic forces; but in reality, the attempt to apply sharp distinctions between good and bad sides, and between intervention and counter-intervention, is likely to be immensely frustrating and endlessly controversial. The tragic case of the war in Vietnam is a case in point; present-day El Salvador offers the same difficulties.

The second major disagreement is over whether interventions to promote democracy or self-government are legitimate or not. Walzer, in his book, adopts J. S. Mill's argument, namely that it is legitimate to intervene for self-determination, but not in order to establish democracy. Mill's argument is that freedom from tyranny is something which one has to fight for oneself; one cannot receive it from the outside. In addition, self-determination is the only agreed principle of international order: democracy, at this point, is really not agreed. Walzer's position has been attacked by critics who have pointed out that modern governments have formidable means of repression, so that one cannot always wrest freedom for oneself without external aid; moreover, the right of a state to be protected from outside intervention is ultimately based on the domestic nature of that state—on the presumed fit between the government and the governed: when a state has a tyrannical government, it ought not to be so protected. To this Walzer has replied by distinguishing between the right of revolution, which citizens have, and external intervention, which foreigners have no right to perpetrate. One must, however, weigh the consequences even of legitimate interventions for democracy: in a world of self-help they will tend to be both self-serving and triggers of chaos.

The last disagreement is on the subject of intervention (by means other than force) for the promotion of human rights— basic, political, and economic human rights. It is a different issue from the previous ones. What is at issue here is not intervention for establishing the right kind of state sovereignty, sovereignty based on self-determination and self-government. It is intervention on behalf of human rights transcending sovereignty, i.e. interventions to limit the internal scope of the sovereign's power. There are strong arguments for legitimizing collective intervention for the promotion of human rights. After all, states behave externally in a way which is very largely shaped by the manner in which they treat their citizens at home. Also, the legal rights which states enjoy do indeed derive from the nature of domestic relations within the state. The rights of states are not absolute: if a state has various rights in international affairs, it is because there is a certain assumption of a fit between the government and the citizens. There are thus very strong arguments, both prudential and moral, for collective intervention on behalf of human rights. However, there is one formidable argument on the other side. It has to do not with the diversity of cultural practices (real enough, but the question is precisely whether tolerance of diversity must entail the tolerance of violations of basic rights), but with the problem of effectiveness and consequences. In the world as it is, what starts as a policy to promote human rights is likely to degenerate into a political instrument of interstate battle; indeed, if one looks at the evolution of American policy on human rights, one sees that it tends to become one more cold-war tool and one more justification of interventions not so much for the promotion of human rights everywhere, as for the protection of one's allies, even when those allies—to put it gently—stink. This is why the theoretical debate on legitimacy is at the same time a vigorous one, since there is a deep division of views, and also ultimately quite misleading if one moves back from the world of abstractions to the real world, in which moral arguments tend to become used as instruments of battle in a decentralized system of self-help.

Ultimately, the only remedies to the problem of intervention are of two kinds. One is to be a good Utopian; then, the problem becomes very easy to solve. All one has to do is transcend world politics by establishing some form of world government (it is now fashionable to call it 'non-territorial, central guidance' just as it became fashionable not to talk about the state but instead to refer to 'authoritative allocations of values'). If one can abolish the units of world politics and give oneself, in imagination, some collective decision-maker, then the problem is solved because there is no longer intervention—by definition, just as when the British government decides to transfer aid from one region of Britain to another, this is not intervention but economic policy. The other remedy, which will always be partial, is quite simply to try to establish the kind of international system which will provide few opportunities for intervention. At the present time, this requires two conditions. One is the internal strengthening of the various units, most of which are, today, very weak indeed, so that these will have a greater power of autonomous resistance to external penetration and manipulation, and fewer temptations to resort to external intervention in order to compensate for or escape from their weakness. One can try to achieve this through massive economic aid, for instance; still, even if economists knew what the necessary effects of economic aid are, which they do not, strengthening the units is probably beyond anybody's reach, given the nature of most of them, which are either formidably artificial or, as in the case of India, face such enormous problems, like population control, that it is very hard to see how the outside world can cope with the task. The second condition for having an improved international system is a relative ideological disarmament of the main competitors, and that seems to be very far away. Given that conditions in the world are likely to endure for a very long time, intervention has only too bright a future.

NOTES

1   Raymond Aron: *Peace and War. A Theory of International Relations*, Weidenfell and Nicolson, London, 1966.

2   Henry A. Kissinger: *A World Restored*, Houghton Mifflin, Boston, 1957.

3   Michael Walzer: *Just and Unjust Wars*, Basic Books, New York, 1977; 'The Moral Standing of States', *Philosophy and Public Affairs*, Spring 1980, vol. 9, No. 3.

3

Intervention and
International law

ROSALYN HIGGINS

To those who are not international lawyers, it may seem very unlikely that international law has any real relevance to the question of intervention.

It is apparent that intervention can mean many different things to many people. It is perhaps less obvious that there are also very many different views about what international law is. If one views international law simply as a static set of rules formulated in a bygone age then it is apparent that it can have nothing to say on the contemporary problem of intervention. But if one perceives it, as I do, as a dynamic process of authoritative decision-making,[1] then it will be seen that it is very relevant to the current attempt to identify and promote acceptable limits to the impinging of one state's activities and interests upon another state's. Rules are really only the accumulated body of past decisions,[2] which, while an essential starting-point, tell us little about variables and still less about changing circumstances. The preferable emphasis is on international law as continuing process, a flow of legal decision-making. It is necessary also to say something about the sources of international law, so that we understand why it is appropriate to draw on particular materials in this context. International lawyers perceive the source of international law, (that is to say where we look for international law), as comprising treaties—multilateral and bilateral, but importantly multilateral treaties; custom, which is the habit evidenced in state practice of doing something through a period of time with the belief that one is obliged to act in that way; and judicial decisions.[3] Each of these is relevant in the context of intervention. It is also arguable that decisions of international organizations are a source of international law whether as state practice or as a special distinct category.[4] But that is more controversial because quite often these decisions emanate from bodies which do not have the authority to bind their members, and consequently one looks to them not as 'rules' or 'judicial decisions' or even 'quasi-judicial decisions' but rather as part of this flow of state practice which can generate custom. They form an important part in the story we have to tell about international law and intervention.

Is there an acceptable definition of intervention in the context of international law? One perceives very rapidly that not only is it not profitable to seek such a definition, but that really one is dealing with a spectrum. This spectrum ranges from the notion of any interference at all in the state's affairs at the one end, to the concept of military intervention at the other. And if one is choosing to deal with all of these as intervention, that choice is immediately complicated by the fact that not every maximalist intervention is unlawful and not every minimalist intrusion is lawful. One cannot simply indicate a particular point along the spectrum and assert that everything from there onwards is an unlawful intervention and everything prior to that point is a tolerable interference, and one of the things we put up with in an interdependent world. It is not that simple. The purpose of the international law doctrine of intervention is, it seems to me, to provide an acceptable balance between the sovereign equality and independence of states on the one hand and the reality of an interdependent world and the international law commitment to human dignity on the other.

Let us return to this idea of the spectrum, and look first of all at minor non-violent intrusions upon the interest and assertions of sovereignty of the other state. The whole question of intervention of a non-military character is closely tied up with international law notions of jurisdiction. An unacceptable minor, non-military intrusion is a violation of a state's jurisdiction. It is universally accepted that a state has jurisdiction over events and persons within its territory.[5] That is known to international law as the territorial basis of jurisdiction. It is not regarded as an infringement of sovereignty or as an interference in a foreign state's affairs to assert jurisdiction over that foreign state's nationals when they are on one's own territory. Territoriality is not the only basis of jurisdiction, however. Other alternative bases of jurisdiction do give rise to questions of unacceptable interventions. For example the United States relies much more heavily than we do on the notion of 'impact jurisdiction'. It is prepared to assert jurisdiction over foreign persons outside of its own territory if the acts they are engaged in have an adverse impact within the United States; their extraterritorial antitrust law is a classical example of this.[6] And this is much resented in the United Kingdom and our recent Trading Interests Act[7] —which many lawyers think a singular piece of legislation[8]—is in my view an altogether excessive and inappropriate response to that difference of perception about what is and is not tolerable in this context.

We have spoken of minor intervention really being a problem of jurisdiction. The other side of the coin is that there exist exceptions from territorial jurisdiction which would be regarded as an unwarranted intervention in the public functions of the state—even though normally one can exert jurisdiction over the nationals or events concerning a foreign state within one's own territory. International law requires restraint if that assertion of jurisdiction would intrude upon the public functions of the other state; and it is for that reason that we have the law of diplomatic privileges and immunities[9] and immunity for foreign states in our courts when they are acting *qua* government.[10]

The term 'intervention' only has a meaning measured against the question 'intervention against what?' and the answer has to be 'intervention against a state's domestic jurisdiction'—that is, intrusion upon that which is for a state alone. But what *is* a state's domestic jurisdiction is a relative matter, and changes through time. A celebrated international law case that came up before the Permanent Court of International Justice, the *Tunis–Morocco Nationality Decrees Case*, contained some very interesting statements about the relativity of domestic jurisdiction and international law and the ability of the line dividing the two to shift through time.[11] We see no better example of this than the area of human rights where we feel free to speak about all sorts of events occurring within the territories of other states, to bring pressure, indeed to exercise certain sanctions and coercion, when in bygone years those would have been regarded as matters essentially for the jurisdiction of the state concerned.

There is a wide range of minor intrusions upon a state's sovereignty carried on through a variety of methods. The diplomatic weapon is obviously extremely important in this context. A state normally has total freedom to establish diplomatic relations with another country or not; but when that weapon is used in a collective form such as the United Nations, one then gets not so much a collective recognition policy but rather a collective non-recognition policy where the diplomatic weapon is used as a form of sanction (a non-military sanction) against a state as a mark of disapproval of its particular policies. The case of Rhodesia was a very clear example,[12] as has been the call of the United Nations for the non-recognition of the South African bantustans of Transkei, Bophuthatswana, and Venda.

Trade presents many problems in the context of minor intervention. Again, one starts from the proposition that any state is free to trade with whomsoever it wants, and indeed free to terminate any trade arrangements that it has; but the reality is that expectations are built up over trade patterns— when trade patterns continue for a period of years expectations about the future are built up, and it is thus an over-simplification to say that one could therefore cut such relationships off at will. This dilemma too is reflected in contemporary events. For example, when the United States introduced its own arms and then subsequently the other forms of export bans to Iran after the taking of the hostages, it is not commonly realized that current contracts were in fact fulfilled. It was only future contracts that were prohibited, but it was regarded—at least on a unilateral basis without a Security Council directive—as inappropriate to terminate existing arrangments even in the extreme circumstances of that time. There has to be a very substantial military background (for example, the Middle East war forming the background to the 1973 Arab oil embargo) before these expected patterns are cut off without any notion of unwarranted intervention. But when one state can legally terminate trade with a prior partner, then definitionally others can join it in doing so. Parallel unilateral action then takes on the appearance of joint action and, again, most countries in responding to the hostages episode in Iran and to the USSR intervention in Afghanistan drew the line after existing contracts had been fulfilled.[13] Trade sanctions, of course, arise as collective diplomatic sanctions in exactly the same way as do the other forms of diplomatic sanctions, such as non-recognition. They are mentioned in Article 41 of the Charter under which trade sanctions are permissible when ordered by the Security Council, when there has been a finding of a threat to the peace, breach of the peace, or act of aggression. The difficulty arises when there has been, for example, a failed resolution at the UN—one that has not been passed because of the veto of a permanent member of the Security Council; and then an attempt to take that same form of sanction that the veto of the resolution would have authorized. The United States, for example, called upon its allies to take with it exactly those measures that were vetoed in the Security Council by the Soviet Union in connection with Iran. And that clearly gives rise to some difficult legal problems.[14] On the one hand there is a resolution that has not gone through; on the other hand there is the proposition that if one country can decide not to trade then several countries can decide jointly not to trade. I think it is right to say there are no clear-cut answers here but rather a delicate balancing act.

Another area of non-military intervention that has become of major importance in the last couple of decades is the question of capital investment and economic influence as an intervention in the internal affairs of a country. This phenomenon, which in a different context is spoken of as neo-colonialism, is closely tied in with contemporary ideas of intervention in the non-military sense. The argument runs that economic influence to that degree can distort the economy; it can lead to the support of one local political party over another; it can have unwarranted influence on the government. This range of problems is not really dealt with by the law of intervention as such at all, but is rather dealt with by a body of law that international law compendiously terms the law of permanent sovereignty over natural resources. That body of law[15] clearly connects the freedom of countries to develop and exploit their own natural resources with the doctrine of non-intervention on the part of other states. A brief survey of some of the leading contemporary instruments illustrates the way in which that relationship has developed. The useful starting-point is the resolution 1803 (1962) on permanent sovereignty over natural resources, which provided *inter alia* that peoples and nations had the right to permanent sovereignty over their natural wealth and resources, and that this right must be exercised in accordance with the well-being of the state concerned. That was followed within a decade by a further series of resolutions which spoke in terms of the efforts of the developing countries and of the peoples of the territories under colonial and racial domination and foreign occupation in their struggle to regain effective control over their natural resources.[16] And more recently there has been the so-called Charter of Economic Rights and Duties which seeks to lay out in some detail the acceptable balance in this area and the detailed articles of that Charter which is a General Assembly resolution. Article 1 states that every state does indeed have the sovereign inalienable right to choose its economic system 'without outside interference coercion or threat in any form whatsoever';[17] so the interrelationship is clearly there.

A further area of interest is that of intervention and human rights. Human rights have shifted from being a matter traditionally of solely domestic concern into a matter of legitimate international concern. We thus now have a situation where other parties are entitled to raise complaints in all appropriate forums without any charge of intervention being reasonably raised against them. There are of course problems about what human rights are, whether some are more 'basic' than others, whether the list is not ever expanding, and so forth.[18] This is not the subject-matter of this essay. But what we can say in the context of our discussion on intervention is that certainly once a human right appears in treaties it then acquires international status, and it is no intervention in the state's domestic affairs to criticize its performance in relation to that obligation. There are many such instruments today, ranging from the UN Declaration on Human Rights to the UN Covenants, which are binding instruments for the parties to them, to the UN Convention on the Elimination of All Forms of Racial Discrimination.[19] But the idea that human rights are essentially still a domestic matter seems to die extraordinarily hard, and a surprising number of western politicians seem to share the Soviet view that mere verbal concern is tantamount to intervention. For example, Enoch Powell, writing about Soviet failures to implement the human rights provisions of the Helsinki Final Act said, in an article in *The Times*: 'The whole policy of Helsinki, Belgrade and the rest is a hair-raising absurdity. The relationship of the Russian state to its subjects has remained unchanged ever since the Russian state emerged . . . to try to shame or cajole or negotiate the Russian state into abandoning these convictions is like standing by the Volga inviting it to be so obliging to flow north instead of south.'[20] Now, of course, Mr Powell makes a fair point in inferring that the Soviet Union could not implement human rights and survive in its present form. But at the margin there is always room for improvement, and there are obviously considerable differences between various Communist countries in the implementation of different human rights, as there are in the western democracies. Freedom of movement, for example, is substantially greater even now for the citizens of Hungary than for the citizens of the Soviet Union. Where I think Enoch Powell is simply wrong is in believing that the treatment of its citizens is a matter only for the country concerned. Human rights have long since passed, by all the conventional criteria that I have identified, into that realm which is of legitimate international interest. We now have a variety of international instruments which actually institutionalize the possibility of states intervening in these areas. The Helsinki Final Act itself, while not technically a treaty, provides for review of progress by continual meetings between heads of state. The eastern European countries continue to contend that the aspect which is written into the Final Act itself is an unwarranted intervention in their domestic affairs, notwithstanding that it is something to which they have given their signatures, along with the substantive rights there.[21] And under the European Convention on Human Rights we have most unusally, a system whereby one state can now bring an action relating to a human rights violation in another

state that does not even concern its own national.[22] That is a
considerable step forward in the diminution of old ideas about
what was and was not unacceptable intervention. The
doctrine of sovereignty has here been restricted to accommodate growing notions of human rights.

While examining this end of the spectrum on intervention a
brief word is appropriate about non-military intervention and
the United Nations itself. The key problem here is that of the
celebrated domestic jurisdiction clause in the Charter—
Article 2, paragraph 7. Article 2(7) provides that nothing in
the Charter shall authorize the United Nations to intervene in
matters which are essentially within the domestic jurisdiction
of a state. It goes on to say that this provision shall not
prejudice enforcement measures. Thus once there has been a
threat to the peace, breach of the peace, or act of aggression, a
finding of that by the Security Council, and a call for
enforcement measures, then the state can no longer protect
itself by claiming domestic jurisdiction. Intervention by the
United Nations at that juncture becomes entirely lawful. But
short of that situation, what acts are unlawful intervention?
What is the status of general (i.e. not specifically directed)
resolutions about affairs that do concern internal matters of
states? Are they unlawful interventions? Certainly the practice
of the United Nations over the years has indicated that they
are not. And indeed, specific resolutions directed at individual
states have been widely tolerated as a legitimate method of
bringing pressure upon a state and yet not falling foul of the
prohibition against intervention in Article 2, paragraph 7.
One is led very near to saying that most things short of actual
action by the United Nations are in fact now permissible
interventions.

I now turn to the other end of the spectrum, the military
aspects of intervention. The starting-point for any international lawyer must here of necessity be the two articles of the
Charter—Article 2, paragraph 4, and Article 51. Article 2(4)
is the basic prohibition against the use of force. That clause
provides that all members shall refrain in their international
relations from the threat or use of force against the territorial
integrity or political independence of any state or in any other
manner inconsistent with the purposes of the United Nations.

That must be read together with the limited permission that the United Nations gives for the use of force by individual states. Article 51, which identifies self-defence, provides that 'nothing in the present Charter shall impair the inherent right of individual or collective self-defence if an armed attack occurs against a member of the United Nations'. Then it goes on to provide that the Security Council shall act to take measures to maintain international peace and security. The prohibition against the use of force is balanced by the permission to engage in individual or collective self-defence. But individual and collective self-defence appears to be limited to armed attacks, whereas the prohibition clause is drafted more widely. Article 2(4) prohibits the threat or use of force against the territorial integrity or political independence of a state. The two sides of the coin do not entirely match. There has been a tendency among most international lawyers to interpret the phrase 'if an armed an attack occurs' quite widely, so as to allow a certain measure of self-defence by way of anticipatory self-defence where the need appears to be 'instant and overwhelming and leaving no choice as to alternative means'.[23]

Now in this area of military intervention, as well, there has been a series of UN resolutions, which again are General Assembly resolutions and not technically binding. For example, there has been the Declaration on Friendly Relations between Nations[24]—a Declaration which was the outcome of several years of legal negotiations, and not a hasty political compromise. The Declaration attempts to elaborate the Charter articles on the use of force. It proclaims the principle that the use of force constitutes a violation of international law, and proceeds to the principle concerning the duty not to intervene. No state or group of states has the right to intervene directly or indirectly for any reason whatever, in the internal or external affairs of any other state. Consequently armed intervention and all other forms of interference or attempted threats against the personality of the state, or against its political, economic, and cultural elements are in violation of international law. The Declaration proceeds to provide that no state may use or encourage the use of economic, political, or other types of measures to coerce another state, in order to obtain from it the subordination of the exercise of its sovereign rights. No state shall organize, assist, foment, finance, incite, or tolerate subversive, terrorist, or armed activities directed towards the violent overthrow of the regime of another state. Though this resolution was arrived at after many years of negotiating, there are very few states which take seriously what is in it. Those from one political corner read in an implicit exception as regards finance and support of armed activities directed towards another state, when these armed activities are those of 'national liberation movements' over-throwing colonial or alien government. And certainly many states regard it in practice as entirely acceptable to bring various pressures to bear, to influence the internal or external events of other states. One thus has constantly the problem of identifying the reality, and measuring it against the rhetoric.

One of the most interesting and difficult areas has been the question of humanitarian intervention and international law. Again our starting-point has to be Article 2(4) of the Charter. Is a state entitled to intervene in another state, by the use of force for humanitarian purposes?—for example, rescue its own citizens or indeed, more unusually, to rescue other citizens, or to rescue 'kith and kin' in difficulty? Article 2(4) of the Charter clearly prohibits the use of force against the territorial integrity or political independence of a state, and it also contains the 'catch-all' prohibition 'or in any other manner contrary to the Charter'.

Article 51 only allows the use of force in self-defence. Is rescuing one's nationals abroad really what is meant by self-defence? The case law indicates that to be rather doubtful. The leading cases on this bring me to the view that the only thing one can do is to try and make a contextual case-by-case appraisal of all the circumstances.[25] The so-called interven-tion at Mogadishu seems not really an intervention at all. The rescuing of the persons on the hijacked aeroplane there, while implemented by external elements, was none the less carried out with the consent and indeed at the request of the host state; we call it 'intervention' at our peril.

The case of the rescue of persons on a hijacked plane in Cyprus is a more difficult case. On the one hand, the Cyprus government certainly was not acting as 'host' to the terrorists in any sense—and indeed was endeavouring to negotiate for the safe release of the hijacked persons—but on the other hand it had set its face against military action. And when military intervention by the Egyptians occurred, there was in fact a loss of life and a great deal of resentment by Cyprus. The facts make this incident fall in a different category.

The case of Entebbe is on its own facts very much clearer. Here the government was undoubtedly supporting the hijackers, and not engaged in any attempts to secure the release of the hijacked persons. In those circumstances it seems to me there is at least a case to be made that an 'in-and-out action' by a foreign state is lawful, and does not in any real sense infringe the territorial sovereignty or political independence of the state. (I appreciate that any brief intrusion is, at the formal level, really an infringement of the territorial sovereignty.) But the point is that one cannot read legal texts as if they tell one all the answers, regardless of the factual context in which they are to be applied. The text has to be applied contextually in any given circumstances, looking at all the variables. None the less, the Entebbe action by the Israelis was categorized by the Secretary General of the United Nations as 'a flagrant aggression'.[26] I have some difficulty in understanding how he could reach that conclusion so decisively.

Yet another problematic case arose from the holding of the United States hostages in Iran. There the state itself was, as it were, the hijacker, and all alternative means of redress had been tried over a very significant period of time. The United States had been at pains to go to the Security Council, and then the General Assembly, and then the International Court of Justice, and to try economic sanctions, before it was finally moved to attempt military intervention. The great difficulty, even if one is prepared to look at this problem relatively and contextually, is that it is extraordinarily hard to see how it ever could have been successful on an 'in-and-out' basis. It is difficult to see that the hostages, held in the Embassy compound, could have been rescued simply by a lightning swoop that would not have been in any extended sense an intrusion upon the internal affairs of Iran. One imagines that the action would have involved some form of overthrowing or restricting of the government concerned. And the other great difficulty was that the intervention occurred in fact while the matter was before the International Court of Justice, of which an Advisory Opinion had been requested.[27] One can only surmise that this happened because of military advice as to the most appropriate moment for the intervention, since until then the Americans had been so painstaking about using, very systematically, the non-military route. The International Court of Justice was clearly very disquieted about it. The International Court was not asked about the intervention—it had simply been asked about the lawfulness of the taking of the hostages. But in giving its reply to that legal issue it did take the opportunity to say that it felt it inappropriate to have to be answering that question against that particular military backdrop.[28]

Finally, we come to the question of intervention and civil war. When one is dealing with military intervention in the context of Article 2(4) of the UN Charter, one is really simply dealing with the lawful and unlawful use of force. To call it 'intervention' is simply a value-laden way of saying it is an impermissible use of force. Care should be taken about doing this in any lawyerish context, however. For example, the Declaration on the Definition of Aggression[29] makes it clear that 'aggression' is not 'intervention'. 'Aggression' involves the military use of force and the unlawful military use of force. 'Intervention', as we have seen, is a term used to describe a spectrum of intrusions—some major, some minor, some lawful, some unlawful. One has to guard against using these phrases loosely and in an identical sense. 'Intervention' in the military context has some reality to the international lawyer in the context of humanitarian intervention, and in the further context of participating at some level in civil wars, in internal wars. The traditional classical international law has it that once the insurgent party in a civil war has reached a certain standing, the status which affords it the right to be regarded by the international community as a belligerent (that is to say it has effective control over substantial parts of the territory and an organized fighting unit) requires third parties to be neutral in their relationships with each of the warring factions.[30] The reality is vastly different. Indeed, there is evidence that the law is perceived differently today. The constitutional government will often itself ask for outside help. It will say that as the constitutional government it is indeed entitled to ask for help. The insurgents will themselves ask for help on the grounds that they are engaged in a battle for self-determination, or to overthrow an undemocratic government or a government that has been engaged in repression of human rights, or they will say they are entitled to recognition as the government perhaps of a ceded part of the territory.[31] Looked at from the perspective of the outside states which have to respond to these requests to intervene, there are many arguments that can reasonably be adduced in favour of supporting the existing government. First of all, they will be able to argue that what is going on in the country concerned is at the moment mere insurgency, mere rebellion; it has not reached that level where neutrality is required. (But conversely, the responding state must bear in mind the growth of the contemporary doctrine of the right of self-determination. If a government is always entitled to ask for the assistance of an outside power it is hard to see the right of self-determination as a reality in the hands of a fighting secessionist or other rebellion movement.) Secondly, it is said that arms may continue to be sold to the lawful government provided that the belligerency has not been recognized. And sometimes it seems to be thought that it is perfectly appropriate for arms to be sold to recognized governments virtually regardless of the status of the rebels. For example, the then Secretary of State for Commonwealth Affairs, speaking in the House of Commons on the Biafra episode, which objectively appeared to fulfil the criteria of a fully fledged civil war, said neutrality was not a possible option for HM Government at that time. Britain might have been able to declare itself neutral if one independent country was fighting another, but this was not a possible attitude when a Commonwealth country with which we had long and close ties was faced with an internal revolt. Such neutrality, he said, would not have been understood or appreciated by other Commonwealth countries.[32] This is strikingly different from the traditional understanding of international lawyers, and one cannot help but notice that really all the arguments militate towards intervention. One hears that one is under a treaty obligation to sell arms to the lawful government, and that it will be a hostile act to cease supply once war begins—including an internal war. One hears that it is necessary to intervene because in fact the insurgents themselves are being assisted by other states so that some form of balancing act is needed. And indeed, as regards the Nigeria question one heard it argued that it was necessary for us to intervene on behalf of the government because the government itself was being assisted by those we did not regard as our allies. And at the political level it is frequently contended that it is necessary for a superpower to intervene because an internal war is occurring within that power's sphere of interest. The realities all militate in favour of intervention. And the task of the international lawyer over the next few years is surely not to go on repeating the rhetoric of dead events which no longer accord with reality, but to try to assist the political leaders to identify what is the new consensus about acceptable and unacceptable levels of intrusion. We have seen from the things I have said about the non-violent part of the spectrum of intervention that international law *can* accommodate itself to changes here. It should not be impossible for us to be prepared to adapt ourselves to these new tasks. Having said that, there are clearly no easy answers, and indeed in so many of these areas international law cannot itself provide the answers; it can only assist in formulating answers when there is a sufficient political consensus to move towards that. But international law is part of and not extraneous to the current debate on the limits and control of intervention.

NOTES

1 See Higgins, 'Policy Considerations and the International Judicial Process', 17 *International and Comparative Law Quarterly* (1968), 58.

2 See McDougal, 'Law as a Process of Decision: A Policy-Oriented Approach to Legal Study', 1 *Natural Law Forum* (1956), 53; McDougal, Lasswell, and Reisman, 'The World Constitutive Process of Authoritative Decision', 19 *Journal of Legal Education* (1967), 253.

3 Along with general principles of international law and (as a subsidiary

source) the writings of leading jurists, see Article 38 of the Statute of the International Court of Justice.

4 See Higgins, *The Development of International Law through the Political Organs of the United Nations*, ch. 1; Castaneda, *Legal Effects of United Nations Resolutions* (1969); Asamoah, *The Legal Significance of the Declarations of the General Assembly of the United Nations* (1960); di Qual, *Les Effets des Résolutions des Nations Unies* (1967).

5 For example, Brownlie, *Principles of Public International Law*, 2nd edn. 290–8; Mann, 111 *Receuil des Cours* (1964), vol. 1, pp. 9–162; Akehurst, 'Jurisdiction in International Law', *British Yearbook of International Law* (1972–3), 145.

6 As exemplified in the Sherman Act of 1890, 15 USC, ss. 1–7 (1976); and the court applications thereof, e.g. *American Banana* v. *United Fruit Co.*, 213 US (1909), 347; *United States* v. *Aluminium Co. of America Case*, 148 F. 2d 416 (2d Cir. 1945); *Timberlane Lumber Co.* v. *Bank of America*, 549 F. 2d 597 (9th Cir. 1976).

7 *Protection of Trading Interests Act*, 1980.

8 See e.g. Tsoris, 'Section 6 of Great Britain's Protection of Trading Interests Act: the Claw and the Lever', 14 *Cornell International Law Journal* (1981), 457; and Huntley, 'The Protection of Trading Interests Act 1980—Some Jurisdictional Aspects of Enforcement of Antitrust Law', 30 *International and Comparative Law Quarterly* (1981), 213.

9 See for example, Vienna Convention on Diplomatic Relations, 500 UNTS 95; Denza, *Diplomatic Law* (1976); and Hardy, *Modern Diplomatic Law* (1978).

10 The common law has recently moved from absolute immunity to qualified immunity, i.e. immunity only in respect of *acta jure imperii*. See Higgins, 'Recent Developments in the Law of Sovereign Immunity in the United Kingdom', 71 *American Journal of International Law* (1977), 423. This immunity is affirmed in the 1978 State Immunity Act.

11 *Tunis–Morocco Nationality Decrees Case*, PCIJ Series B, No. 4.

12 Security Council Resolution 216 (1965), 12 Nov. 1965; Security Council Resolution 277 (1970), 18 Mar. 1970 (Rhodesia); General Assembly Resolution 2775E (XXVI) 29 Nov. 1971; General Assembly Resolution 3411D (XXX) 28 Nov. 1975; General Assembly Resolution 31/6A, 27 Oct. 1976 (Bantustans).

13 See e.g. 5th Report Foreign Affairs Committee, House of Commons, para. 36; Higgins, 'Legal Responses to the Iran Crisis', *Proc. Am. Soc. Int. Law* (1980), 250.

14 Higgins, op. cit., *supra* n. 13 at 251.

15 On which there is now a vast literature. For an introduction, see Schachter, *Sharing the World's Resources*; Brownlie, 'Legal Status of Natural Resources in International Law', *Receuil des Cours* (1978), vol. IV, 249.

16 General Assembly Resolution 1803 (XVII), Dec. 14 1962; General Assembly Resolution 3201 (S-VI), May 1 1974.

17 General Assembly Resolution 3281 (XXIX), Dec. 12 1974. See especially Article 2 thereof for a detailed statement on the treatment of foreign investment.

18 For a thoughtful analysis of some of these questions see Bilder, 'Rethinking International Human Rights: Some Basic Questions', *Human Rights Journal* (1969), 557. See also McDougal, 'Human Rights and World Public Order: Principles of Content and Procedure for Clarifying General Community Policies', 14 *Virginia Journal of International Law* (1974), 387; and Milne, 'The Idea of Human Rights: A Critical Enquiry' in *Human Rights, Problems, Perspectives and Texts*, ed. Dowrick (1979).

19 660 UNTS 195 (Racial Discrimination Convention); UN Doc. A/810 (Universal Declaration); European Treaties Series No. 5 (European Convention on Human Rights); 6 *International Legal Materials* (1967), 360, 368 (Covenants on Human Rights).

20 *The Times*, 24 June 1977.

21 See Henkin, 'Human Rights and Domestic Jurisdiction' in *Human Rights, International Law and the Helsinki Accord*, ed. Buergenthal (1977).

22 Article 24 European Convention on Human Rights provides for interstate complaints.

23 The test enunciated in *The Caroline*, Moore, *Digest*, vii, 919.

24 Declaration on Principles of International Law Concerning Friendly Relations and Cooperation among States in Accordance with the Charter of the United Nations, 9 *International Legal Materials* (1970), 1292. See furthur Ronzitti, 'Resort to Force in Wars of National Liberation' in A. Cassesse (ed.), *Current Problems of International Law* (1975).

25 For different views on the problem of humanitarian intervention, see Lillich (ed.), *Humanitarian Intervention and the United Nations*; Brownlie, 'Humanitarian Intervention' in *Law and Civil War in the Modern World* (ed. J. Moore, 1974), p. 217; Frank and Rodley, 'The Law of Humanitarian Intervention by Military Force', 67 *American Journal of International Law*.

26 See, *inter alia*, Paust, 'Entebbe and Self-help', 2 *The Fletcher Forum* (1978), 86; Salter, 'Commando Coup at Entebbe: Humanitarian Intervention or Barbaric Aggression', 11 *Int. Lawyer* (1977), 331.

27 *Case Concerning U.S. Diplomatic and Consular Staff in Tehran (USA v. Iran)*, *ICJ Reports* (1980).

28 Ibid., paras. 93–4.

29 Resolution on the Definition of Aggression, 13 *International Legal Materials* (1974), 710.

30 Lauterpacht, *Recognition in International Law*, and Castren, *Civil War*.

31 Higgins, 'Internal War and International Law' in *The Future of the International Legal Order*, eds. Falk and Black.

32 Hansard, 27 Aug. 1968, cols. 1146, 1443–4.

4
Superpower Intervention
PHILIP WINDSOR

It is fashionable, at present, to suggest that the old Westphalian system of a world of non-interventionist states is on
the decline, and that the dangers of growing intervention by
different powers in the affairs of other states have been on the
increase. The Westphalian system represented some remarkable achievements: the absolute sovereignty of a state rested
on a dual basis whereby internal authority was matched by
freedom from external interference; and in this way the
principle of *cuius regio eius religio,* codified in the Religious
Peace of Augsburg, laid the foundation of the modern state
system. Today, these achievements are regarded with a degree
of nostalgia, and there is a widespread assumption that the
current threats to the system represent something new. Yet if
one looks at the recent history of the world, it seems that this
non-interventionist system of sovereign states, providing
states with the domestic freedom to conduct their own affairs
as badly as they like, is in many respects rather stronger than
it used to be. At the height of the imperial era, or even in the
1920s, states which failed to pay their debts were liable to be
bombarded by their creditors. Today a state in default merely
asks for a reschedule. Its creditors meet, grant it more money
to pay even more interest on further debts, and the nearest
anyone comes to interference is that the International
Monetary Fund might lay down conditions for a substantial
advance. This applies not merely to a case like that of Poland,
but also to countries in Latin America, the Middle East, or the
developing world. The non-interventionist system is still
strong in many respects and its strength has indeed increased.
But at the same time a general assumption persists of a world
so dominated, indeed permeated, by sheer power that it
becomes almost futile to discuss the question of intervention
by the superpowers because it is like asking what contribution
oxygen makes to our ability to breathe in the atmosphere.

The ability of the superpowers to influence others, their reach, the extent of their interest in so many parts of the world and in so many of the areas of the lives of other countries, constitute, one might be tempted to think, a fundamental and permanent form of intervention, even a kind of structural intervention affecting the activities of all kinds of other states in the world. In this sense, then, can one talk about superpower intervention with any degree of specificity? Is it not just a general condition—or is there such a thing as a form of intervention distinctive to superpowers? Are there ways in which superpowers intervene and are their forms of intervention symmetrical, are they like each other, and unlike those of other countries? Questions of this nature raise several other questions along the way, and I propose to examine some of them, in trying to turn back towards this first, that of whether there is such a thing as superpower intervention.

First of all there is the question of the degree of superpower freedom to intervene, and along with it that of whether the superpowers are becoming more or less free to intervene, not only in terms of their relations with the rest of the world but in terms of their relations with each other. These two initial questions then raise a third, whether the superpowers intervene in like manner and for similar reasons, or in unlike manner and for different reasons.

Now, their freedom to intervene is partly restrained by common inhibitions about their own strength, and their need to avoid crises with each other. The sense that they are inhibited by the fear of approaching anything like a nuclear war; the common constraint which in different ways they both acknowledge; these do suggest that the superpowers very frequently feel less free to intervene than other countries do. If one considers, for example, the recent history of Zaïre, one can see that on the one side Cuban forces were able to advance what they took to be their cause in the province of Shabah, and on the other that French and Belgian troops dared to intervene, but that neither the United States nor the Soviet Union felt audacious enough to engage in direct action. In this sense the degree of inhibition which constrains the superpowers can often hold them off from intervention, as if they were like poles repelling each other in a magnetic field. Very often they are less free than many other countries might be. Indeed, one could almost suggest a scale of intervention which would show that the greater the power of a country, the less free it will be to use it, and that it is small states like Israel or Vietnam which can get away with anything, while very big states like the United States or the Soviet Union are simply constrained and inhibited.

But beyond this question of their mutual restraint and their mutual constraint there lies another which is that of whether they have begun to create a system whereby they do not intervene. Such a system depends not only on the ultimate threat of nuclear war, but on the intermediate steps of trying to avoid a nuclear war. In other words, it depends on the assumptions which lie behind the doctrine of Mutual Assured Destruction. The difficulty, however, is that MAD has enshrined a basic paradox ever since it became yet another acronym of the nuclear age. From its beginnings in the mid-1960s it has been susceptible of interpretation in one of two ways. It can mean that the prospect of nuclear war is so appalling, and that it is so paramount a necessity to avoid its dangers, that all powers must collaborate in avoiding the kinds of conflict which might otherwise bring them to the brink of hostilities. So, in this interpretation, the superpowers collaborate in the elimination or regulation of conflicts which might otherwise have been exceedingly dangerous. One might indeed argue that roughly from 1969 to 1973 the two superpowers reached a whole series of agreements, not only on regulating the arms race itself, but on helping to avoid or regulate conflict in the Middle East, on the status of Berlin, which until that time had been potentially a very risky issue, and on other matters. In general they acted in such a way that their attempts to regulate the world implied increasing co-operation and even perhaps a degree of joint superpower intervention in some areas of conflict, notably in the Middle East. But their activity certainly implied no individual superpower intervention of the kind which might have led them to war. MAD in this sense became a way of avoiding, of regulating conflict as far as possible, in order to eliminate the dangers of nuclear war.

On the other hand it could be interpreted quite differently.

It could be argued that because destruction is mutually assured, because both parties know that there would be no winners of a nuclear war, it is very unlikely that either side will go to the extreme of attacking the other. In that case nuclear war can be more or less discounted, providing that the system is maintained and a second-strike capability exists; since nuclear war is unlikely to erupt the world is now safer for conflict, powers can afford to engage in adventures, and can afford forms of intervention which in the recent past looked much more dangerous than they do today. Thanks to the beneficent workings of MAD the possibility of intervention or adventure, of engaging one's forces in different areas of the world, has actually increased. In that sense MAD can mean, and I would argue has come to mean, greater scope for superpower intervention than obtained previously.

Roughly after 1973, in the place of the agreements and understandings which characterized the years after 1969, one can discern a growing disposition towards superpower intervention; a growing assumption that the safety of the world now permitted of conflict, and in that sense a growing tendency towards adventure. This might apply particularly to the Soviet Union and its activities. Certainly over the past three or four years, it has shown an increasing disposition to intervention: either by proxy, as in the case of Vietnam and Cambodia, or by the direct use of advisers as in the case of Ethiopia, or by a combination of both in parts of Africa or in South Yemen, and of course, most directly of all, in Afghanistan. In this sense there has been a growing spate of Soviet interventions particularly since 1978, and much of such activity can be attributed to the way in which the Soviet Union has interpreted (not being alone in doing so) the workings of MAD: as conducive towards renewed or even increased intervention in the future. So the paradox of MAD, that it can be interpreted as a procedure for avoiding conflict altogether, or one of shaping a world which is safer for conflict and intervention, seems to have been resolved by a growing disposition to intervene.

This disposition has been somewhat held in check by the United States by an attempt to re-create a military threat; in other words, by the formulation of a global containment policy, of which such instruments as the Rapid Deployment Force are one expression. If intervention can be dangerous after all; if it were to raise the possibility of war, even of nuclear war; if even a Secretary of Defence, James Schlesinger, declared that limited war was possible when deterrence failed at one level, or a Presidential Directive 59 invoked the idea of a controlled nuclear war; if in short the feasibility of nuclear war is restored, then it is possible to think once more in terms of containment. But if the prospect of increasing intervention in a world made safer for conflict can only be inhibited by evoking new dangers of nuclear war, then we are going down a very dangerous path indeed. I would also suggest, however, that neither superpower has shown any real inclination to go anywhere near the edge of a nuclear war; in consequence the possibility of a world which is open to an increasing degree of superpower intervention is one which we must now contemplate.

Now, if the superpower relationship is one which now permits of greater intervention than in the past, what kinds of intervention are involved? Clearly, forms of pressure—of exercising influence and leverage over other countries—are the stuff of international relations in any circumstances. Clearly, economic inducements to behave in a certain manner, or political pressures, or diplomatic *aides-memoire* do not really constitute intervention. This is the way in which most states seek to conduct their relations most of the time, and one does not have to be altogether a partisan of what is nowadays called the 'rational actor' approach to the study of foreign policy, to suggest that none the less states do generally see their interests in comparable ways, try to maximize their influence, and do what is in their power to ensure that other states fall into line. Whatever their degree of power, they evoke power as an instrument for their purposes. In such terms, intervention should not be characterized by such criteria as the giving or withholding of a loan. Moreover, such practices are very often self-defeating if they are used as forms of intervention.

Economic sanctions, for example, have seldom worked in history, and where they have, as perhaps they did in the case of the transition from Rhodesia to Zimbabwe, this was not because the economy crumbled but because the gradual wearing down of the economy allowed the emergence of a rather stronger guerrilla force than might otherwise have been the case. Sanctions in fact very seldom work directly and most other forms of economic pressure, when applied as sanctions, are equally ineffective. The recent history of Poland is a case in point—unless one interprets the activities of General Jaruzelski since the imposition of martial law as those of a clandestine agent for the International Monetary Fund and the bankers, as opposed to those of a leader operating on behalf of his own national interest. In this sense, the notion that economics or propaganda constitutes intervention is a misreading and over-extension of the word intervention. Such are the normal forms of activity in international relations.

What, then, is intervention? It must refer primarily either to the use of military force by one country against another, or to the deliberate encouragement of force, be it terrorist or electoral, in the society of one country by an external power, either with gold, or with propaganda, or with arms. Such intervention has occurred fairly frequently. The history of Portugal since 1974 suggests that the reason the Social Democrats achieved a somewhat unexpected triumph did not derive from Portuguese politics only; it was also due to the fact that Western European social democrats, headed by Olaf Palme and Willy Brandt, gave support and money to the Portuguese Social Democrats to counter what the Soviet Union was also providing for the Portuguese Communist Party. To some extent this is intervention; it is an attempt to influence the internal affairs of one country, or the choices it might make, by external means, whether by money, propaganda, or the supply of arms. In such a sense, there is a considerable record of superpower intervention. But this is not intervention on the same level or in the same frame as intervention in terms of the direct overthrow of a regime, or direct subversion, or the direct use of military force.

Many people in Europe, not only 'Euro-communists', tend to regard such latter forms of intervention—invasion, direct interference, the direct or indirect overthrow of regimes, in a somewhat symmetrical way. Does the Soviet Union invade Czechoslovakia and overthrow a government there? Shortly afterwards many people would find a parallel in the way that the United States destabilizes a government in Chile. 'Destabilization' is one of the more admirable euphemisms invented by Henry Kissinger to describe such American activities, and I remember a cartoon in the French press, shortly after the fall of the Allende government in Chile. It simply showed a cross bearing the name Allende and a wreath bearing the name Dubcek. In this sense one does tend to see these forms of overt or violent intervention by the superpowers as parallel and symmetrical. But are they? That becomes a question of the levels of intervention, and the rationales behind it. I would suggest that there are ways in which the two superpowers do act in a certain parallel sense; there are also ways in which their activities are far from symmetrical.

The way in which they do act in a parallel sense comes from the idea of a special superpower responsibility. That is a phrase much beloved of some of the spokesmen of American administrations, and again particularly associated with the name of Henry Kissinger; but it is also one taken up in certain Soviet pronouncements to mean that: 'We superpowers have a special responsibility for avoiding nuclear war.' This is the obverse image of my original contention that the superpowers were often inhibited by the fear that they might find themselves drifting towards a nuclear war. But this obverse image also suggests that the avoidance of nuclear war has become a prime duty in the maintenance of international order. That the two countries which are capable of starting and waging the kind of nuclear war which could destroy the globe, now have not only an overriding interest but also a kind of new legitimacy in the exercise of their power—which demands that they should ensure that any other conflicts of whatever kind do not lead to an all-out confrontation between East and West. Since in fact it is only the two superpowers themselves which are capable of starting the kind of nuclear war which could destroy the world, this is really a circular argument. They have the power, therefore they are responsible, therefore they must have the power to go on exercising their responsibility. In one sense, it is cant but since it is equally impossible for either of them, at least up to now, to reach any agreement on how to devolve their power or how to reduce the level of power to the point where they might not in fact destroy the world, it does also signify an active duty to try to maintain a world in which they do not use their power and thereby destroy it. In consequence, this special superpower responsibility has tended to mean that they can sometimes intervene after all. Consider, for example, the history of the war in the Middle East in 1973. This was not only a war which was made possible by direct intervention, that is to say by the supply of vast quantities of arms, and indeed of money, it was also a war whose conduct was characterized by active and continuing intervention on the part of both superpowers. They were engaged in co-operation at the same time. Both wanted to win the peace: equally, both were determined that neither of the local powers should win an all-out victory. In consequence, the United States was intervening as much against Israel in the later stages of that war as it had been intervening for Israel in its earlier conduct. The Soviet Union was consistently intervening against Israel, but it was not always intervening for Egypt, it was rather trying to secure a particular outcome. In this sense the superpower responsibility and the special duty, enjoined upon them by themselves for the purpose of avoiding nuclear war, also meant that they were engaged in a very variable pattern of continuous intervention designed to achieve a certain kind of outcome. Even though they were not coming into conflict, they were competing none the less for an outcome which would regulate the conflict which they could now envisage. In such ways 'responsibility' can lead to direct intervention not because it is primarily characterized by past troubles, although it might be, but because of the need to avoid a nuclear conflict. And yet, if they secure such a world of order; if they achieve what one might call a state of legitimized intervention—legitimized by the higher interests of avoiding a nuclear holocaust—then they can, of course, continue with their power struggles. And in this sense such struggles do continue: through influencing the outcomes of wars, through the ability to intervene, by proxy or more directly by supplies, or even possibly by direct involvement. The proviso is that the power struggle is maintained at a level which does not threaten to topple over into a risk of nuclear confrontation.

Examples are legion, but a good one, I suppose, might be

that of the Bangladesh conflict. It appeared that the United States had decided that future relations with China were more important than the immediate question of the outcome of the war; while the Soviet Union had maintained its support of India. As the war drew to its climax the United States, aligned to some degree with a Chinese-backed Pakistan, was concerned about the possibility that Bangladesh might be entirely submerged by Indian forces. Intervention then began to develop. The United States dispatched an aircraft carrier up the Bay of Bengal. Suddenly, a number of members of the Soviet Politburo were summoned home from places as far apart as Vladivostok, the Crimea, and Stockholm. Very shortly, units of the Soviet fleet began working up the Bay of Bengal as well. The possibility of overt intervention was rising steadily at this point. It was not designed to achieve a particular outcome, as was the case in the 1973 war, but was designed to perpetuate a particular power balance in the Asian subcontinent. In the end, nothing happened. The conflict was resolved without the active participation of either Soviet or American forces. But one could observe a power struggle developing from which, if it had not been resolved, a limited conflict could have emerged, conducted at a lower level than that of nuclear confrontation.

Generally, then, special responsibility at one level can go hand in hand with power struggles at another level. But the difficulty clearly lies in keeping them apart. Does the power struggle begin to threaten that special responsibility, that legitimacy of world order, which the two superpowers have taken it upon themselves to maintain? Then they encounter a major inhibiting factor at the same time. They might conduct their competition; they might threaten active intervention; they might feel able to outsmart one another; or to get there first, or to try to influence a particular ally in a particular way at a well-chosen moment. But they might equally conclude that such behaviour is too dangerous, that the level of conflict can very rapidly spill over from that of straightforward competition to that of major power struggle and high-level risk. In such situations they do not intervene—as in Zaïre, where they leave it to Cubans or East Germans, and to French and Belgians. At such moments, they are still inhibited by the very extent of their power, and even by the extent of their interest. Overall, then, the consequence is a primary form of superpower intervention, characterized by the maintenance of international order: one which unites the superpowers in a common purpose, that of avoiding too high a level of risk, but which also enables them to continue with their power struggles, and to maintain the possibilities of intervention, at a lower level of risk.

But there is a different kind of intervention, and in respect of that one might argue that questions of public order do not arise, and that the legitimacy which is evoked is of a higher and different kind. What does the Brezhnev Doctrine say to the countries of Eastern Europe in 1968? It categorizes certain principles—proletarian internationalism, socialist construction, the leading role of the party, and so on—which must be maintained if the socialist commonwealth is to survive, and it makes clear that these principles override the norms and boundaries of international law. The Soviet Union will feel free to intervene in the affairs of a particular socialist country if it considers that the principles of socialism are being violated and that the security of the socialist commonwealth as a whole is thereby threatened. This is not anything like the public law which, one might argue, underlies the first form of intervention. *That* after all, is concerned with maintaining some stability in an international order which would otherwise be very dangerous. In this sense the 'public order' aspect of stability might be said to be something which the Soviet Union has picked up from the United States, although frequently it has also used it to legitimize its own activities, in terms which the United States would not welcome. But the other level is not that of public order at all, it is very like a medieval doctrine. In fact, Colonel Draper of the University of Sussex once produced an analysis of the Brezhnev Doctrine in terms of the medieval ideas of natural law; and they do bear a striking similarity. The activities of princes can be overriden by the decrees of the church; and the terms of just war, the terms of what natural law implies about the moral conduct of human affairs, become the basis of public order. The Brezhnev Doctrine is similarly an appeal to an overriding moral or historical principle, claiming a higher legitimacy than that of international law. In this way the Soviet Union came forth with a doctrine which legitimized for the future any actions it might undertake, any forms of intervention in which it might engage so long as it felt that fundamental principles were at stake. Now this is an exercise not merely in maintaining an empire or in avoiding risk, it is an exercise in the interpretation of history and in the creation of a higher legitimacy. The Soviet Union, after all, is engaged, at least in theory, in a long historical struggle; a struggle which is a deliberate attempt to change the world; a struggle which draws its legitimacy from the past in the sense that it depends on historical analysis. It is determined by a philosophy of history and its transformations, of the derivation of the 'ought' from the 'is', and of how such a derivation will lead to a certain conclusion in the future. But while it is based on the past it can in fact only be tested in terms of future activity. The Soviet leaders are unimpressive as Marxists, if not as Marxist-Leninists, but none the less, the Marxist principles are still embedded in the way that the Soviet Union directs its activities and justifies them, and one of the fundamental Marxist principles at stake is that of praxis.

That implies more than the question of what can be derived from theory or from philosophical interpretation: it declares that theories are actions themselves, that until they are actions they are not even ideas, and that in this sense the question of understanding the world does indeed become that of changing it. In consequence, the historical analysis becomes a demand upon the present and the future. So the way in which the Soviet government interprets history—even officially—also means that it has engaged itself in a task of applying history to the future of the world. Such an application of history, when it is not brought up short against the overriding need to avoid nuclear war, in other words when it does not come into direct conflict with the 'public order' principles of superpower responsibility, can supersede the other principles of public international law. The Soviet Union, in other words, has created a higher order of legitimacy for intervention. Now, is this peculiar to the Soviet Union?

It could be argued that just as the Soviet Union has picked up from the United States some of the public order notions of special responsibility in the avoidance of nuclear war, so the United States also has reacted in some respects to the Soviet Union in framing its own category of super-legitimacy. After all, American governments will justify much of their activity in Latin America in terms of the need to defeat Communist subversion. The 'last, best hope of mankind' sees itself as the custodian of an idea of freedom, of a way of managing affairs, and of directing how other nations should manage their affairs, precisely because it also confronts the threat of Communist subversion—or in other words, the Soviet Union's attempt to translate its history into the present. And the United States can also appeal to an overriding, a universalizing principle to justify different forms of activity. One might take for example the sometimes politically damaging but otherwise relatively innocuous and perhaps, on occasion, even admirable crusade for human rights. The United States has clearly regarded itself as entitled, and indeed enjoined, to make an issue of human rights in its relations with other countries. In some respects, of course, there is an obvious entitlement. A country signatory to the Helsinki Final Act of 1975 is entitled to draw the attention of other governments to the fact that they are not obeying its provisions or even observing it, and conferences are duly convened in Belgrade or Madrid to open up the discussion. There is no question but that such exchanges are perfectly legitimate in any terms of international law, and indeed of international order. The United States has the *right* to draw attention to violations of the Final Act among the signatory countries. But under President Carter America went beyond the confines of the Final Act. It addressed the question of human rights in many different contexts, some of which were embarrassing because they involved allies like Iran, or because it was difficult to raise such subjects with countries like China if at the same time the State Department was trying to draw the Chinese into a closer relationship, or because for similar reasons the claim was made of progress in Brazil when there was none. So the universal became particularist and selective. Yet, for all that, one can observe the pretensions to a higher legitimacy in the human rights campaign. 'We, the Americans, in our defence of freedom, and by virtue of our mission in the world to represent a new alternative to the old societies of Europe, have the right to tell other nations about the way they are conducting their affairs and whether they should or should not proceed along the same lines.'

But there is more involved here than a particular American position. The American form of a higher legitimacy also derives from the combination of power and mission which the United States has had thrust upon it, and has increasingly welcomed in the years since 1949. It derives from the fact that the United States was the centre of power in the world, at a time when, for many years, there were practically no other centres of power: Washington combined economic and military power of an order never before seen, and that led to a vast extension of political influence in very many parts of the world. The United States had assumed a particular and historically unique role: that of defending other countries against a universalizing foe. Communist intervention, Communist subversion, or Communist attack led it to intervene, as in the case of Greece. Because it had to extend its protection to these other countries, the American role in combining legitimacy and power gave it, as it were, a right to speak for a universal cause: that of freedom on the Western model. In that sense the United States, too, had a historical task, and it has continued to maintain it. It claims a *right* to intervene in order to protect other countries against threats from outside, yet its intervention purports to be directed towards the specific *and* universal end of maintaining freedom anywhere. The rhetoric of President Kennedy's inaugural address—'To bear any burden, fight any foe, to sustain the cause of freedom',—encapsulates the American role, and the American claim to legitimacy too; the higher legitimacy of the American disposition to intervene in other parts of the world. This had disastrous effects as well as, on many occasions, beneficent ones. The most disastrous was clearly in Vietnam where the United States continuously increased the scale and scope of its intervention throughout a succession of governments long after the one which had originally invited any association with the Americans in the first place had been forgotten, and after the principal ally of the United States in South Vietnam, President Diem, was overthrown partly by

American efforts. All the same, the scale of American intervention increased until finally, almost as unilaterally as it had committed troops to combat in the first place, the United States decided also unilaterally to withdraw. In this manner intervention which had originally taken the form of fighting in Vietnam now took, by the end of the story, the form of a decision to withdraw from Vietnam: it certainly was not made with the prior agreement of the South Vietnamese government.

Here, too, is a case where a higher legitimacy prevails over international public law; and in such cases, the two powers find themselves locked in a kind of perpetual claim to a historical task historically justified in terms of the present and the future, and in which the roles of both are mutually reinforcing. I am suggesting here that the United States really acquired its role by reaction to the Soviet Union, because it perceived Soviet threats around the world, but that thereafter what has happened is that each superpower has continually reinforced the other in the terms by which both are able to justify these interventions. Each will declare 'I am able to intervene not only because I have a historical task but because you also are intervening. You are threatening the world order which I represent and which I know to be the true one'. So these mutually exclusive claims to a particular kind of future; the expectation that each does represent the victor in the future struggle: these attitudes also mean that intervention becomes a mutually self-reinforcing exercise on the part of both superpowers. The higher legitimacy ultimately suggests that even though all the arguments for order, all considerations of caution and constraint still remain in force, there is still a constant impetus towards continuing intervention.

Moreover, this latter impetus has been reinforced by the relative *weakness* of both powers. If one looks at their historical expectations around the late fifties and early sixties, one can discern in both cases a certain assumption that the world was going their way. The United States certainly had some grounds for believing that more and more countries were going to be influenced not only by American technology and economic power, but by the modernization which technological and economic change would bring. The process of modernization, it was confidently predicted by many Americans, and most eloquently perhaps by Walt Rostow, would naturally induce other countries to model themselves more and more on the Western pattern. In other words, as a particular society modernizes, so it also Westernizes. The culture and the values change. There was, of course, some reason to believe this. Clearly, many countries cannot modernize without changing culture and values. A green revolution might not make much difference, but an efficient agricultural system might change the whole nature of land tenure in a particular country. The continual process of subdividing land in a certain society might also be bound up with marriage customs, for example; and this could mean that an attempt to produce more food could mean not only a change in the system of land tenure, but also a revolution in social structure and very often in social values. What this implies, however, is that modernization does *not* mean Westernization; it only means change, and change can produce severe crises. Crises can also take the form of violent reaction againt American power or American intervention. In such circumstances, the approach typified by Walt Rostow can hardly survive developments like those in Iran in recent years, where it was precisely modernization which endangered the cohesion of society, and also brought about a violently anti-American reaction. In the end modernization presented a challenge and a change, but did not produce Westernization. But the original expectation was that history, through the economic, technological, and social impact of the United States on the world, would naturally Westernize it, and that it was really a matter of time.

The Soviet Union was equally confident of its own historical success in this same period. The Soviet view tended to the belief that the anti-imperialist forces were advancing, that they were natural allies of the Soviet Union, and that even though they had many historical stages to go through before approaching socialism, the 'bourgeois nationalists' were the natural allies of the USSR and would doom the forces of counter-revolution and imperialism to defeat. Again, there was something to be said for this view. A great many newly emergent countries, recently decolonized, did go through a period of strong anti-Western feeling, sometimes translated into anti-Western politics. In some cases, certainly, they looked to the USSR at this time; and Soviet rhetoric, combining the higher legitimacy and the practical politics, dwelt at length on the issues of just wars, national liberation, and so on. But again the USSR has witnessed the failure of these dreams. It does not find that bourgeois nationalists are its natural allies. On the contrary, articles occasionally appear in the Soviet press, notably one in *Kommunist* in 1978, which declare in effect that the Soviet Union has had its fill of bourgeois nationalists. 'They have treated us with rank ingratitude. They do not respect the Soviet Union, have exploited it, and then discarded their helpers'—just as any red-necked Congressman might inveigh against foreign aid. In this sense, the Soviet Union was arguing that it needed 'ideologically reliable allies', those who were prepared to model their society, indeed their revolution, on the Soviet pattern.

Such arguments reflected the failure of the Soviet Union, which mirrored the failure of the United States in a particular way: namely, that the natural processes on which both counted—economic and social transformation in one case, the ideological and political workings of history in the other—were disappointed. The question then arises whether their parallel disappointment would prompt them to a greater degree of intervention—a greater degree in the name of historical legitimacy as opposed to the public order. The answer here seems inconclusive. Recently, the United States has been more actively intervening in Latin America, for example, than was the case under President Carter. Events in the Western hemisphere suggest that the United States is active in terms of the drastic categories which I suggested at the beginning. Those not just of economic influence or political propaganda, but those of military supply and military influence as well. It seems equally true to suggest that the Soviet Union has been active in its search for ideologically reliable allies since 1978. If one considers that year, one sees the Soviet Union finally changing sides between Somalia and Ethiopia and consolidating its relations with Ethiopia. One sees a treaty of friendship with the People's Democratic

Republic of the Yemen which provides the USSR with a permanent role in that country, as well as bases and facilities. It is also in that year that the Daoud coup in Afghanistan begins the long process of Sovietization of that country, and also at the end of it, that the ideologically reliable Vietnamese take on the ideologically unreliable Khmers Rouges in Cambodia. One cannot relate all these events to a single article in *Kommunist*; each development has its own antecedents on the ground as well; but it is interesting that at the time the Soviet magazine declared that the USSR's natural historical expectations had been disappointed it did adopt a more interventionist approach. One might, therefore, draw a correspondence between increased disappointments with history and an increased degree of intervention. But how far is it possible to extrapolate from such conclusions to the future?

That question cannot yet be answered. The constraints of the system are still powerful and the ability of the two powers to manipulate other countries without encountering the risk of confrontation with each other is still very high. I would suggest that there has been a greater tendency towards more active intervention over recent years than in the past; none the less such tendencies are still subject to many of the constraints which have operated throughout the nuclear age.

So far I have argued that there are two primary modes of discussing intervention. One is that of the public order, dominated by the need to avoid nuclear war, which endows the superpowers with the self-justifying ability to manipulate and intervene. The other is that of the higher legitimacy of the historical task, which produces occasions on which the public order arguments do not necessarily prevail. But all this implies a certain symmetry; and I suggested earlier that one of the questions involved is whether there is indeed a symmetrical pattern, or whether the behaviour of the two powers should not be differentiated. Now, clearly they differ ideologically. The United States does embrace an ideology of pluralism, of the open society and the free market, which suggests that, at the governmental level at least, the United States is disposed to be a much less interventionist power than the Soviet Union. Arguments concerning the activities of multinational corporations need no rehearsing here, and they do sometimes have governmental support, but on the whole their activities cannot be categorized as governmental, or as forms of direct national intervention. I think it is true to say that its ideology does make the United States a less interventionist power than the Soviet Union, whose ideology is, after all, concerned with the creation of a particular social order. The Soviet Union regards and declares itself as the custodian of that order. But the asymmetry goes further than different ideological approaches. There is a more fundamental asymmetry, which is implied in the Brezhnev Doctrine. That doctrine itself expresses a form of structural intervention, which goes on all the time. I am speaking not only of the Brezhnev Doctrine itself here, but of the entire Soviet relationship with Eastern Europe. The Soviet Union does not have to intervene very often by direct action in Eastern Europe because it has already been intervening all along.

Contemporary American analysis of developments in Poland at the end of 1981 was often superficial, tending glibly to suggest that they resulted solely from Soviet machination; even so, one American Senator did have a point when he asked 'But how can the Soviet Union be intervening in Poland? It has been intervening every day for thirty-four years'. A structural intervention does characterize the affairs of Eastern Europe and such behaviour is unique to the Soviet Union. There are a number of titularly sovereign states, whose political system is dominated by one consideration only: that of how far we can go before the Russians call a halt. They have considerable leeway, for the ambiguities of the Brezhnev Doctrine are marked and allow a fair latitude of interpretation, so that under cover of accepting its principles they can interpret, for instance, socialist construction in many forms of economic experiment. They can emphasize the leading role of the party, but combine it with a kind of unofficial pluralism—provided it does not become too official. They can pay lip-service to proletarian internationalism but disagree quite openly with many aspects of Soviet foreign policy. In these respects I would not suggest that Eastern European states are all under the heel of the Soviet Union, but I do suggest that everything they do is measured constantly by considerations of how the USSR will react, and how far it will allow them to go. In this sense, a structural intervention does persist in Eastern Europe—stronger perhaps in the past, but still strong in the present—and it also creates a complex set of reactions for the nations of the West.

For the implications are that the Soviet Union enjoys two different kinds of hostage in Europe. First it has hostages in the West, based on the military vulnerability of Western Europe. It is this hostage Western Europe which influences American policy through the Europeans' concern about their own vulnerability and the need to avoid policies which could lead to war. That was highly effective for many years, particularly at the time when the Soviet Union was weaker than the United States in other dimensions of strategic power. But since a relative liberalization has come about in Eastern Europe, that area has emerged as a second hostage. Here the message is that the Russians did not intervene in Poland, at least not directly; that they allow economic experiments to go ahead elsewhere; that the Soviet Union has been very circumspect in its dealings with Yugoslavia, and has more generally shown a degree of restraint in its dealings with all of Eastern Europe. The West, therefore, should not provoke it into doing anything rash or tyrannical. *Détente* in Europe should be preserved as far as possible; and this is a universal prescription on the part of European statesmen, not confined to Helmut Schmidt and Giscard d'Estaing, who became notorious for repeating the incantation. In this sense, hostage Eastern Europe provides a way of ensuring that the West cannot react too strongly to other forms of Soviet activity elsewhere. Does the Soviet Union invade Afghanistan? Then the West should be cautious in reacting lest Poland is invaded too. So the second hostage constitutes not only a form of structural intervention in Eastern Europe itself, but also in-surance against the Western powers' reacting in any consistent or coherent manner to Soviet activities elsewhere which they regard as threatening, or which do constitute intervention. So the very fact that the West has a powerful, emotional, and even political interest in Eastern Europe means that the Soviet Union now enjoys a certain advantage.

It might be argued, however, that there is still a pattern of symmetry to be discerned here. One could maintain that just as the Soviet Union is engaged in structural intervention in Eastern Europe so is the United States in Latin America. There are some good American studies on this question, which have brought out interesting parallels between Soviet behaviour in Eastern Europe and American behaviour in Latin America. It seems true, though, to say that while the United States has certainly been an active interventionist power in Latin America for very many years, and that while it does have a powerful economic stake there, its ability to intervene in the continent is all the time declining. In the smaller Latin American countries, as for example in Nicaragua, where the United States first intervened and then desisted, or in a case like that of El Salvador, where active intervention continues, this might seem absurd. Clearly the United States still has great power in such countries. But it seems equally true that other countries, such as Venezuela or Mexico, are perfectly capable of pursuing policies which the United States regards as inimical in ideological terms, or radical in OPEC terms; yet the threat of American force is not invoked. Their activities are not conditioned by the fear of an American reaction in the way that Eastern European activities are conditioned by the fear of a Soviet reaction. One cannot imagine a Poland in some kind of Eastern European energy consortium behaving as Venezuela has done in OPEC.

One should beware of making facile assumptions of symmetry. Between the two superpowers, there exists not only a difference in ideology but also a difference in conduct. There is also a difference in their geopolitical circumstances. Latin America is not anybody's hostage to anything; Eastern Europe *is* a hostage to other considerations, including Western European values. In this way, the position of Eastern Europe is radically different from that of Latin America.

While, therefore, one can discuss the superpowers at a certain common level, and they do exhibit certain common forms of intervention, they are rather different animals, and the ways in which they behave cannot be presented altogether symmetrically. But one should add that the problems of what constitutes superpower intervention are certainly likely to grow. The historical disappointments; the different expectations; the need to maintain control in a world which is becoming very much more difficult to control; the fact that the centres of power that once were all found in Washington have now been dispersed in so many ways in Western Europe, Japan, and China; the fact that such different *centres* of power now operate different *forms* of power: all these considerations make it harder to maintain order in the world. It is also true that many governments now find their own societies harder to control, so that now it is very much more difficult even for a superpower to ensure that what another government promises, it can perform. A superpower, concerned at the level of public order in a world which is slipping out of control and might breed more conflicts, is likely to contemplate intervention, if need be, in order to reimpose control. Both superpowers might consider it in common, and in that sense they cannot avoid a certain role. When Chairman Mao once said that China would never become a superpower he did so, I think, not only because China would find it difficult to become one anyway. He was also referring to the nature of the superpower role in the world—one which China emphatically rejected and which he became conscious of by studying the activites of the superpowers themselves. Stuck with their position, but unable to achieve sufficient collusion to rule the world, as it were, by a Soviet–American condominium, yet obliged to avoid the dangers of a nuclear confrontation, they are unfortunately liable by reason of their caution as well as by that of their power to remain prone to intervention for many years to come.

5
Intervention in
French Foreign Policy
DOMINIQUE MOÏSI

On 24 May 1978, *The Times* carried an article entitled 'We used to behave like the French'. The second Shaba operation had just taken place and it was apparently with a mixture of bafflement and envy that the other European nations, especially those with a colonial past, reacted to this spectacular high point in what could be described as a pattern of intervention in French foreign policy. It is highly symbolic that in this series centred on the theme of 'Intervention in World Politics', France should be the only country, apart from the Superpowers, to be singled out by the dubious honour of a specific chapter dedicated to her—an honour that was not bestowed on the shoulders of well-known interventionist countries such as Cuba and Libya. It is, I believe, a legitimate honour since intervention has played a key role in French foreign policy, and its significance is crucial to a global understanding of France's attitudes toward the world and of France's own self-image.

I intend to start with some preliminary definitions, so as to circumscribe the specificity of French intervention. I will try to analyse the nature of the relation that existed between France and francophone Africa, i.e. the reasons why part of the African continent constituted a privileged territory for French intervention. I will ultimately attempt to define the characteristics of French intervention.

If one takes intervention in its classical legal definition, i.e. 'dictatorial interference in the internal affairs of another State', which I intend to do to grasp the specificity of the French case, French intervention as such, in spite of its symbolic importance, is dually limited in time and in space.

One cannot really speak of intervention before 1960, the year of achievement of independence by the French African

states, or 1962 and the end of the Algerian war. The war in
Indo-China, the war in Algeria and, more generally, French
military action in the Maghreb cannot be described as
interference in the internal affairs of another state, since they
were colonial struggles within the French territory or the
French empire. Even the unhappy Franco-British intervention on Suez in 1956 can historically be described as the last of
the truly European colonial operations, an unsuccessful and
anachronistic attempt to replay the Crimean War, a hundred
years later. It is nevertheless important to assess what the
Suez affair represented for France. The Canal take-over by the
Egyptians jeopardized, of course, substantial economic interests, since about 48 per cent of French oil supplies came
through the Canal. Moreover, some eighty thousand French
investors held about half the shares of the Canal Company.
Yet, deep antagonism to Nasser was the prime factor in
French policy. For the French, to dispose of Nasser was a way
of defeating the Algerian rebellion. Beyond that, there was the
urge to wipe out the memory of a succession of humiliating
failures: the defeat of 1940, Indo-China, Morocco, and
Tunisia. The French desperately needed a victory to bolster
their self-esteem. Interviews made at the peak of the Suez
crisis are highly revealing of that state of mind. What were the
French élites saying? 'We are trying to turn history back . . . to
wipe out the strains of Munich which led to our defeat in 1940,
and of our failure to prevent Hitler from taking over the
Rhineland in 1936 . . . Nasser is the symbol of all France's
enemies . . . of all France's humiliations in the past.' [1] The
Suez affair, in its deep psychological motivations, but also in
its final result, the humiliation of the old European powers
both by the superpowers and the new Third World leader is of
great symbolic importance. Together with the Indo-China
and Algeria wars, the Suez crisis translated France's
reluctance either to abandon its empire or to stop playing an
imperial role.

The Suez crisis played an accelerating role in the French
decision to build an independent nuclear weapon, but it acted
as a moderating force in limiting the scope and therefore the
geographical extent of French intervention. From then on,
French intervention would be circumscribed in space to

Francophone Africa—French police intervention in Mecca in 1980 involved no more than ten French gendarmes used, if one may say, on a 'consultative' basis.

The other direct military presences of France—in Lebanon under a United Nations peace-keeping force, or possibly in the future in Sinai in an *ad hoc* European force, or the stationing of French troops in Germany—do not belong to the same category. French troops are present in these cases in compliance with an international treaty and within the framework of international agreements—even if France's acceptance to perform such a function reveals French willingness to have a world—and not only a regional—role.

But let us come back to our definition of intervention, 'a dictatorial interference in the internal affairs of another State'. So described, the French policy of intervention corresponds to the encounter between a specific set of circumstances, those of the African continent, its natural weaknesses aggravated by the legacy of decolonization, and in particular the artificiality of its divisions in too many States, but also the closeness of the cultural links between France and francophone Africa, and a specific ambition, that of France. That ambition is a mixture of idealism and cynicism, of sense of duty and outright exploitation of the weaknesses of others, and corresponds to a desperate and somewhat successful attempt to refuse to adapt, and yet to adapt at the same time, to the international system after 1945 and France's newly reduced international status.

France's claim to independence, the building up of an independent *force de frappe*, coming out from the integrated military body of NATO and the maintenance of close and privileged political, military, economic, and cultural links with francophone Africa are the two pillars of a single policy, of the very claim to international existence. Independence, as conceived by the French, and intervention are therefore closely linked. One may consider them both as comfortable pretexts. What can the meaning of independence be, for a middle-size power such as France after 1945, in an increasingly interdependent world dominated and divided by the superpowers? The shrewd use of a 'nuisance value' policy by de Gaulle on East–West questions has, in that sense, the same significance as the French policy of intervention in Africa. Such a policy of intervention corresponds ultimately to a refusal to accept the diminished sense of self stemming from the loss of an empire.

But the pursuit—and, to a large extent, the success—of such a neo-colonial policy could not be explained without an understanding of francophone Africa, of the context and the nature of the links existing between local and French elites. France's relations with the African continent date back more than two centuries. Eighteen out of the fifty members of the Organization of African Unity are former French colonies or French territories. If one adds Zaïre, Rwanda, Burundi, and the Mauritius islands, French is the official language in twenty-two states. The élites of these territories have not only adopted our language but, for many, our culture; and some of them have ultimately participated in the political life of metropolitan France before independence. Senghor, Houphouët Boigny, Modibo Keita, were Ministers in the Fourth and even in the early years of the Fifth Republic. One tends to forget that Sekou-Touré was a Vice-President in the National Assembly. All these rulers felt that at least one of their ancestors had been a *gaulois*. These close personal links explain the willingness of the African Governments not to sever the links existing with the Metropole, not only at the economic level with France, and through France with the European Community, but also politically, thanks to the mechanism of the *Communauté* settled by de Gaulle, but well prepared this time by the Fourth Republic through Deferre's *Loi-Cadre* of 1956, which set the ground for political autonomy.

If francophone Africa was an ideal continent, given the French ambition to play a world role, there was also another reason. It was weak and seemed to call for outside interference, one that would not be dangerous for France, because of Africa's relative seclusion from world politics and the superpower rivalry at least until the 1970s. Given the weaknesses of the African nation-states, French military means were perfectly adequate. For the French, to intervene militarily in the Middle East would have been too costly and above our means, as the Suez adventure had clearly shown. Africa, given the archaic state of its armies, was within our reach, a continent ideally fitted for the small interventions in which France specialized, where a light, but necessary counterweight could make a decisive difference.

Not only was Africa within French reach and its leaders willing to accept the preservation of French influence, but the African continent itself had been, from the early colonial days, perceived by the French as a key instrument of French diplomacy. Following France's defeat in the Franco-Prussian war, the conquest of Africa took on the character of a national compensation through which the country could regain its rank in the European concert. It was with Europe in mind that France went to Africa.[2] As a result, the defence of Africa—the largest part of the French Empire—became closely associated with the defence of France itself. This geostrategic association was reinforced during the Second World War, when Africa became a major theatre of operations and a crucial source of manpower and support for de Gaulle's Free French Forces.

After 1946, the Fourth Republic emphasized the role of Africa in rebuilding the Metropole as a great power. In the late 40s and 50s, various French strategic writings stressed the importance of Africa for the defence of Western Europe. They warned that since the Soviet Union was being contained by NATO in the European theatre, it might attack the West through Africa. Red arrows were drawn on maps of the world to show the new grand design of Soviet strategic planners.[3] Therefore when, starting in 1975, intervention by proxy of the Soviet Union took place in Africa, it could be integrated in an old French scheme. At long last, French action could be presented not as a remnant of colonialism through a neo-colonial attitude, but as a responsible Western answer to Soviet imperialistic ambitions, even if the two were compatible.

Let us now turn to the characteristics of French intervention in Africa. First, this policy has been implemented through *ad hoc* institutions, largely outside the purview of traditional diplomatic channels. French intervention in Africa has been a highly personalized, presidential venture, a modern incarnation of the eighteenth-century '*secret du Roi*' which often replaced the official policy of the Foreign Ministry.

Under the Fifth Republic, the decisions have been taken by the President himself with the help of two *ad hoc* institutions, the Ministry for Co-operation and the 'Secretariat Général pour les Affaires Africaines et Malgaches', whose role is to maintain a permanent personal link between the French President and the francophone heads of states. This position was held until 1974 by M. Foccart, and then downgraded to the status of Conseiller Technique, a position held by M. Journiac until his death in 1980. President Mitterrand himself has maintained the position held today by M. Penne. The role of the Quai d'Orsay consisted mainly in selling abroad a policy decided elsewhere, hence its traditional reluctance to support decisions for interventions, as much out of prudence as out of frustration for having been left out of the decision-making process.

A second specificity of France's policy of intervention is its formally legal character. The French have insisted in circumscribing their military interventions under two legal umbrellas: one given by the 'accords de défense', formal bilateral defence agreements that provided for French military intervention conditional upon the request of the local government and at the approval of the French authorities, even if often in reality these agreements were signed when the decision to intervene had already been made. The other 'umbrella' France offered was the military technical assistance agreement (*accord d'assistance militaire technique*) which provided for French aid in the organization, equipping, and training of the national armies and police forces of the new African states.

A third important characteristic of French intervention is its limited scale, especially if one compares it with the size of the current Cuban forces. If one excludes the 4,000 men stationed in Djibuti, which was a French territory until its independence in 1977, there were never more than 10,000 French troops in francophone Africa and never more than 2,000 in one place at the same time and, in most cases, they were there for short periods only. Therefore the expression used in the late 70s, describing France as the Gendarme of the West, must be given a restrictive meaning.[4]

Within this policy of intervention, important distinctions have to be made. One should distinguish between interventions that correspond to purely internal destabilizations, and those that are reactions to external aggressions, even if the origins of the troubles are internal. This second type of intervention is easier to justify in the eyes of the world, because it constitutes an answer to another external intervention.

Historically, most interventions—at least until 1974—were aimed at stabilizing leaders of regimes which had gained their independence from France. The numerous interventions in Cameroun, Congo-Brazzaville, Gabon, Chad, Niger, and Mauritania between 1960 and 1964 fall under this rubric. They were at the time justified by the French on the ground of the need to protect newly created regimes. 'It is not possible that a few gunmen be left free to capture at any time, any presidential palace, and it is precisely because such a menace was foreseen that the new African States have concluded with France agreements to protect themselves against such risks', to quote the Minister of Information of the time, M. Alain Peyrefitte.[5] France's non-intervention was most often also a form of intervention, passivity representing a conscious choice to abandon a disappointing leader. 'Ne pas agir, c'est encore agir', Jean-Paul Sartre would have said. Such was the case with Fulbert Youlou in Congo-Brazzaville in 1963, or with Hamani-Diou of Niger in 1974. Usually, the reasoning behind these non-actions was the lack of credibility of the deposed leader. Looking at the evolution of Congo-Brazzaville and comparing it with the stability of Gabon, where the French intervened to save M'Ba and where his successor Bongo is still in power, some French officials are still wondering whether they should have intervened in Congo-Brazzaville. Non-support to an endangered leader may sometimes take a more active form, as is the case of the Central African Republic, where the French, after having supported—for too long, many people would say—the Bokassa regime, actually intervened to replace him, with the man Bokassa had himself deposed, Dacko. When Africa became, following the Portuguese decolonization, a theatre of superpower confrontation, Soviet-Cuban penetration on the one hand, Libya's African ambitions on the other, the rationale for French intervention shifted from internal to external threats. French destruction of the Polisario columns which attacked Mauritania in 1977, France's recent involvement in Chad and, above all, French intervention in the Shaba provinces of Zaïre in 1978, fell into this second category. French intervention in Kolwezi in 1978, which was undoubtedly a success, had the dual ambition, apart from its humanitarian justification of saving the lives of white civilians, first of drawing a line to further Soviet-sponsored destabilization in a geostrategically key country, particularly since, at that time, no other Western nation, particularly not the Americans, were ready to enter the African struggle, and secondly of reassuring France's clients of her willingness to honour her commitments. French military disengagement from Chad in 1979 endangered, in the minds of many African leaders, the credibility of France's guarantees. In African eyes, Chad was at least partly the equivalent of what Iran represented for the Arab clients of the United States.

At a time when strong Third World nationalism coincides with a certain reluctance in the West to use military intervention, it is remarkable that France's repeated military undertakings of the last few years have incurred so few political costs and have even attained, on the whole, a degree of success. Yet, this policy has its own limits and even contradictions. Diplomatically, if such a policy reinforced French prestige in the West, Belgium excepted, there is clearly a contradiction between French emphasis on Third World and North–South issues, coupled with its claim that the economic dimension of the African problem is the essential one, and France's military practices. Another form of French intervention, the policy of arms sales, has contributed also to a relative isolation of France on African issues. Arms sales to South Africa, which continued on an extensive scale until the end of the seventies, undercover action to help the Biafran secessionist attempt—a perfect illustration of France's will to weaken the Nigerian 'giant' perceived as a potential threat to its small francophone neighbours—have also contributed to explain some African condemnations. Nigeria, a country with which France has clearly had difficult relations, denounced France's intervention in Shaba as a modernized version of nineteenth-century imperialism. For General Obasanjo: 'Just as our ancestors could not accept the gunboats of the last century, we cannot accept the dropping of paratroopers in the twentieth century.'[6] France's own colonial past is a help, but also a limit to its political and psychological margin of manœuvre.

Some situations are also unresolvable, owing to the artificiality of the entity inherited from decolonization. Whatever France's possible error in Chad in supporting 'the wrong man', in a too ambiguous policy *vis-à-vis* Qaddafi, or in a vain and rather naïve belief in the efficiency of an inter-African force, it may well be that nothing can be done to save that country from exploding.

Militarily, whatever the justification of the claim that for France Africa is a 'custom-fitted' continent, and that only small counterweights are needed, France does not have, in terms of logistics, transportation, and communication, the necessary means with which to carry out its modest ambitions without risks. This explains the reluctance of the French military establishment to get involved in new adventures. The Kolwezi operation was carried out thanks to US means of transportation, even if French policy-makers found, in that form of logistical support, an added dissuasive and diplomatic value.

Psychologically, the French are not fully at ease with a policy of intervention whose neo-colonial after-taste is evident, even today—hence, the legal screens behind which the French surround themselves before acting. Public opinion has been passively supportive of France's policy of intervention in Africa, understanding its logic. But how would it react to French military deaths? The political impossibility of risking significant casualties constitutes the most formidable limit to French intervention.

It is not clear whether France under Mitterrand will be able to carry out a global North–South policy beyond generous declarations of intentions, or whether she will continue regional policies with a different tone. Given the nature of the problems involved and France's limited margin of manœuvre, change may be less siginificant than originally envisaged by the Socialists. In Africa, Socialist France is caught between two contradictory objectives: the need to differentiate herself from Giscard d'Estaing's policy with its neo-paternalistic taint, and the need to reassure all those countries whose stability depends on French political, economic, and all too often military support, in what can be considered as the last French sphere of influence in the world.

France's new guiding principles in Africa can be summarized as follows: a desire to widen the French presence beyond francophone Africa, an attempt to de-emphasize military aid while stressing the more 'pure' economic and cultural aspects, and an intent to condemn South Africa more strongly. These principles are new only in their formulation. Giscard d'Estaing had also pursued an active, if unsuccessful, policy beyond francophone Africa. Sensitive to Nigerian criticism and fearing a direct military confrontation with Libya in Chad, Giscard took French troops out of Chad, a move that was criticized in France and in some African countries. It is also important to stress that criticism of South Africa already existed under Giscard, who stopped the sale of arms to Pretoria.

There will be inner limits to France's African policy if only because economic aid will necessarily be limited, her allies will expect military protection, and ties with South Africa will remain exceedingly complex. A lack of available funds may force the maintenance of what amounts to a sphere-of-influence policy. Unfortunately for the idealistic component, these countries are generally not the poorest. Libya's President Qaddafi's growing ambitions in Africa are already leading France toward increasing logistical aid to the regime of Goukouni Oueddei in Chad. The recent withdrawal of Libyan troops is unquestionably a success of French diplomacy. It remains to be seen whether Qaddafi's withdrawal is anything more than tactical, whether a joint African force is enough to preserve a fragile equilibrium, and whether French forces will not once again have to intervene in Chad.[7]

Ultimately, if change occurs, it may be due more to African domestic evolutions. The nature of French intervention in Africa is based on the specific nature of the cultural relationship which existed between France and the first leaders of francophone Africa. The successor generation is bound to have different attitudes with regard to France. This phenomenon constitutes the ultimate limit in France's capacity to pursue a policy which has been so far an undeniable success, but whose limitations are bound to increase with the process of time.

NOTES

1   Herbert Luethy and David Rodnick, *French Motivation in the Suez Crisis*, the Institute for International Social Research, Princeton, NJ, 1956, p. 80.

2   Henri Brunschwig, *Mythes et réalités de l'impérialisme colonial français*, Paris, Armand Colin, 1960.

3   These ideas could be found in particular in the articles published in the 1950s by the *Revue de Défense Nationale*.

4   On these questions, cf. my article with Pierre Lellouche: 'French Policy in Africa: a Lonely Battle against Destabilization', *International Security*, Spring 1979.

5   *Le Monde*, 28 Feb. 1964.

6   *Le Monde*, 21 July 1978.

7   On Mitterrand's African Policy, cf. my article 'Mitterrand's Foreign Policy: the Limits of Continuity', *Foreign Affairs*, Winter 1981-2.

6

Intervention and Access to Natural Resources

EDWARD N. LUTTWAK

Nothing is gained by considering the general when it is in truth the particular that defines the matter: oil *is* a special case, indeed unique—at least for a while. For another decade quite certainly, and perhaps for two, the economic well-being and therefore the social stability and thus the political equilibrium of a hundred countries around the world both large and small will continue to depend on secure and sufficient supplies of oil. All manner of raw materials are freely traded on the world market, and those who would try to control the supply of any one—as the Organization of Petroleum Exporting Countries has done—soon discover that the fluidity of substitution which modern industrial techniques allow limits the gain to a brief interval. And such gain is soon transformed into permanent loss: once a costly synthetic plant or a new non-cartel mine comes into existence, even a prompt reduction in the price of the original product will not easily recapture the lost market.

Under this dispensation, recondite materials now produced by only a handful of countries, and thus seemingly easily cartelized, remain available to consumers at reasonable prices, along with rare metals and common ores, foods and fibres, coal, and virtually every other raw material. Oil is different, not because it is a 'noble' product as the late Shah was fond of saying, but rather because it is so commonly used in such enormous quantities even while its supply is greatly concentrated. It is one thing to develop a tolerable ersatz for tantalum or columbium needed by the pound or the hundred-weight; quite another to replace oil by the million metric tonne. Hence the ease with which the supply of oil has been controlled by the cartel, and its colossal extortion, which since

1974, and more acutely since 1978, has greatly impoverished the world economy.

The cartel does not of course operate with electronic precision. Because there is as yet no substitute for oil on the requisite scale, it is the ability of the world economy to absorb its exactions that serves as the sole limit to the price-setting power of the cartel. Confidence in the will and ability of the cartel to act according to its long-term ('enlightened') self-interest was the crucial ingredient in the optimism of the bankers and economists who have been so active in minimizing the consequences of high oil prices. The cartel would not increase prices excessively, we were told by Robert S. McNamara in his World Bank incarnation and by many others claiming similar authority, because to do so would cause a global economic depression, which would in turn reduce demand for oil—and thus diminish the revenues of the oil exporters. Everything would of course depend on the estimation of very complicated differential elasticities—but for some peculiar reason it was believed that the finest of such calculations would be made in Riyadh, apparently the new seat of higher economic wisdom in place of Cambridge, England and Cambridge, Massachusetts.

Naturally the optimists were wrong, and as of now the cartel is suffering a loss in total revenues since its over-extortion (the 'second oil shock') has damaged the world economy excessively. Thus, at the moment of writing, prices are somewhat reduced so that the barrel of oil which used to sell for less than two dollars in 1972, and which is supposed to be sold for thirty-four dollars by the cartel's order may actually be purchased for a mere thirty. Consequently, the oil-exporting countries have suffered a loss of income which reflects in miniature, and no doubt temporarily, the huge losses inflicted on the world economy ever since 1974, which have been manifest in the form of diminished growth and financial imbalance, along with their attendant consequences: unemployment for those who go out to work and impoverishment for those who do not—the peasants and craftsmen of the poorer countries that have no oil.

One recalls the soothing estimates offered by assorted experts when oil prices began to multiply: scarcely anything would be lost; they claimed growth would be reduced by a percentage point or two for a year or two, and 'recycling', they said, would overcome all the disequilibria in international payments. In the United States especially, many positively welcomed the change. thinking no doubt of Nigeria or Ecuador as the beneficiaries, and of affluent suburbanites as the contributors; the promoters of international economic equality saw the cartel as a most fortunate device that would make the rich a little poorer and the poor a little richer. As for the new but most articulate band of ecologists, they looked forward with pleasurable anticipation to the demise of the eight-cylinder automobiles of vulgar working-class Americans and saw no great loss in a reduced rate of growth that would arrest the spread of mills, satanic or electronic. And if fears were expressed for the financial stability of all the many countries large and small that would suddenly have to pay tribute to the cartel measured in tens and then hundreds of billions of dollars, no less a figure than Robert S. McNamara, head of the World Bank, stood ready to explain with great patience how everything would work out just fine.

What followed of course was the abrupt interruption in the ascent of the poorest in the poor countries to the modest prosperity that tube-wells (with diesel pumps) and fertilizers (oil-based) could provide; the deceleration in the high-growth economies of the hard-working that were reshaping millions of lives for the better in such diverse countries as Brazil, Korea, and Turkey; the recessions and depressions of the highly developed in Europe, North America, and East Asia, and more generally the end of the economic optimism that had propelled the progress of the world economy since the Second World War. While the limousines of the bankers that reassured us back then remain polished and well fuelled, millions have suffered unemployment if not outright impoverishment in the centres of the automobile industry in Europe and North America; while the professional anti-growth ecologists remain no doubt well funded, the 'green revolution' has come to an end in the crowded countryside of Asia.

And what great purpose has been served by the change? Certainly the search for oil has been broadened and deepened (literally so) in many of the newer wells, and certainly much progress has been made in energy conservation. But it seems that these adjustments and also the technological quest for alternative energy sources would have taken place anyway, and altogether less painfully and much more economically had it been only the increasing natural scarcity of oil that would have set the pace of substitution: 'crash' programmes are never efficient even if effective.

As a matter of fact, the very origin of the price increases retarded the process of conversion to other sources of energy. When oil that costs perhaps a dollar to produce in Arabia (by the most inflated estimate) is sold in a market artificially controlled for thirty-four dollars, the would-be investors in very costly substitution industries must hesitate, since they know that the price is rigged and may collapse if the power of the cartel were to be broken. If, by contrast, oil prices had increased steadily and cumulatively in reflection of natural scarcity, oil might now be selling for much less than thirty-four dollars a barrel and yet there might be more rather than less investment in substitution, since risks and rewards could then be projected on the basis of more reliable estimates of future oil prices. The *certainty* of being able to sell substitute energy (including non-OPEC oil) for, say, twenty dollars per barrel is a more powerful incentive to investment than the possibility of fifty-dollar oil—when there is also the possibility of fifteen-dollar oil.

There is thus little merit in the insistent claim that the cartel has actually contributed to the long-term health of the world economy by 'reinforcing' the price mechanism; the peculiar readiness of many commentators to find virtue in the cartel's extortion reflects more the inherent tendency to rationalize and justify evils deemed uncontrollable than any economic realities.

The Case for Intervention

The easier case for intervention, by the classic definition of a 'dictatorial interference in the internal affairs of other states', presumes a deliberate interruption of supplies by producers who collectively control a decisive quantum of production rather than a mere increase in prices. Ever since the 1973 Arab oil embargo, the menace of another and possibly more prolonged and more complete interruption has been a factor in world politics. It is that fear which best explains the peculiar solicitude of many governments for the plight of the Palestinians, a stateless people—to be sure—but one of many, and a nation many of whose members are refugees, but again the world is filled with refugees who benefit from no such eager concern. Anything that attracts sympathetic attention for any part of the large congregation of suffering humanity must be welcomed, regardless of motive, and in spite of a transparent insincerity. But in so far as the fear of another Arab oil embargo is translated into real leverage for the Arab oil producers in world affairs, the latter must expect that it will evoke countervailing leverage. What remains to be defined is the form that such countervailing leverage might take, and specifically the role of force, if other means are destined to be ineffectual. The morality, legality, feasibility, and necessity of the use of force are discussed in what follows.

The Moral Aspect

There is an obvious difficulty in upholding the morality of the use of force in response to an act which comports no violence in itself. It can be said outright that no moral case can be made for the use of force in order to *retaliate* for the imposition of an embargo; there is an obvious disproportion between the resort to deadly violence and the denial of supplies which are not directly and immediately essential for survival. But that is not the circumstance before us: force would not be used to punish the countries that would impose an embargo, but rather to undo its results by seizing oil field to restore production.

Thus the moral issue is defined by a comparison between two sets of consequences: what will humanity suffer if the hypothetical embargo is simply allowed to continue, and what will be the suffering inflicted by an act of intervention designed to restore production and supply? That an embargo both comprehensive and prolonged would inflict great suffering is clear; the catastrophic disruptions that would be manifest in the wealthier economies would translate eventually into increased death rates in poorer countries. When millions of workers become unemployed in the highly industrialized oil-importing countries, thereafter surviving in varying degrees of comfort at public expense and by exhausting private savings, many more millions in 'middle-income' economies will have to survive unemployment without public assistance and with scant savings destined to be soon exhausted; and then in turn the poorer countries, where the very concept of unemployment is irrelevant, will be dragged down from poverty into a worse situation.

It is only by a science yet more dismal than economics that one could arrive at some precise estimate of the deaths that would eventually follow an embargo both comprehensive and prolonged. It is clear, however, that if the oil of Arabia is removed from the market, prices of one hundred dollars per barrel may reasonably be expected for remaining supplies, and that would mean that hundreds of millions of people would remain without the fuel that they need to pump water for their crops, to heat themselves in the coldest weather, to boil water for safe drinking, and to cook food that cannot otherwise be eaten. In the additional malnourishment and sickness that would follow, millions of deaths would undoubtedly result.

As against that, it may be estimated very safely that an intervention conducted in the empty lands where oil is produced in the greatest amount, where local military forces are feeble and where no popular resistance is to be expected at all, might result in a few hundred deaths or at most a few thousand, and even that requires the heroic assumption that an intervention competently staged would evoke serious resistance.

What makes such calculations quite safe is that the combined number of those who would be exposed to life-threatening hardship all over the world must be a hundred times greater than the total population of the countries and mini-states that a forcible intervention would affect. The fact that the first and very large casualty toll would be caused indirectly by a denial of supplies, while the second and much smaller toll would have been inflicted by the weapons of war is morally irrelevant: that distinction is a matter of aesthetics, not ethics.

In the discussion above, the consequences of an oil embargo (comprehensive and prolonged) have, of course, been depicted in the context of the present economic world order. But to argue that none need starve if the hypothetical embargo is immediately followed by a drastic restructuring of the world economy and by appropriately huge transfers of food, medicine, and so on from the rich countries to the poor, defines theoretical possibility to be sure, but not a feasible alternative, and neither does it affect the moral calculus. The complex of traditions and institutions, the distributions of skills and capital which condition the functioning of the world economy are not anyone's deliberate creation, but rather the inherited results of centuries and millennia of divergent development in different parts of the world. To argue that the deadly consequences of oil denial should rather be undone by demolishing and remaking the entire economic structure of international society is equivalent to the argument that theft should be prevented by abolishing private property. To do that would certainly abolish theft, but equally it would soon enough have the secondary result of abolishing property as well, since none would have the reason to bring it into existence by work, accumulation, and saving. Similarly, the attempt to transfer food and the rest on the scale which would be required to undo the deadly secondary consequences of the hypothetical oil embargo would soon enough diminish the supply to the point where a sufficient transfer would be unfeasible.

In any case, moral questions are not to be resolved by the *ad hoc* creation of artificial worlds which transform the terms of the answer. It is within the present world that the injury of oil denial must be compared to the injury of intervention—and by any calculus of suffering, the latter must be an injury far smaller.

The Legal Aspect

I will not attempt to address legalistically the question of legality, preferring to do so instead jurisprudentially. The former course would require an investigation of precedents and conventions as well as an appropriate interpretation of the UN Charter; the latter by contrast requires us to consider the very meaning of legality as it may apply to the case at hand.

It is possible no doubt to construct an argument whereby any and all use of force between states is deemed *ipso facto* illegal, as is already the case for private force in municipal law (wherein the exception of self-defence implies a prior illegality). It is understood, of course, that the illegality of force in municipal law presumes the existence of alternative methods of relief against injustice. In their absence, to prohibit the use of force without prohibiting the exploitation of all non-forcible instruments of power and control, must mean that the world is made safe for all such injustice as such instruments can cumulatively engender. Just as within the municipal sphere, the protection of private property without any restraints on its accumulation brings the population to a state of *de facto* serfdom, except for a relative handful of monopolists and latifundists, so also (in the absence of any other restraint upon it) the cartel would be free to inflict economic damage without any possibility of relief, if the use of force is ruled out *ab initio*. In practice, of course, relief is available in the form of additional substitution and conservation measures that would be initiated or accelerated by the advent of an embargo—especially if its prolonged nature were known from the start. Thus it is not the interruption of oil supplies *per se* which creates the injustice that requires redress, but rather its abrupt character: if the oil exporters were to announce their intention of restricting or terminating oil sales at some date in the future (several years removed), then substantive remedies could have timely effect, and no unredressed grievance would remain to justify the use of force.

One can scarcely conceive of circumstances in which the oil exporters would want to impose an embargo so greatly deferred, and the case has no practical significance, but it does serve to bring to the surface the underlying legal principle which defines the offence and can justify the use of force to reverse its consequences if other means are ineffectual. In selling oil over a long period of time in conditions where no adequate alternative sources of energy are available, the exporters inherently assume the obligation of continuing to sell their oil unless *force majeure* intervenes. The monopolistic seller enters into an implicit contract as well as the explicit contract that attends each transaction. While the latter is negotiated each time anew, the former is latent and fixed, but it still carries an obligation. If, for example, all the food consumed on some remote island is sold by only one shopkeeper, and if the latter were abruptly to refuse further sales without some compelling reason, the islanders would not be judged guilty by any court if they kept themselves supplied by forcibly taking what they needed (against customary payment) until such time as the arrival of other supplies would terminate their need for self-help. The cognizant monopolist (or cartel) tacitly assumes an obligation merely by operating in that context; if the obligation is evaded, an offence results against which force may justifiably be used when no other remedy exists.

That surely is the principle which applies to an embargo. If Arab oil producers were to attempt to use the 'oil weapon', weapons of the ordinary sort might justifiably be used to seize, secure, and operate the oil fields and loading facilities so long as: (i) the embargo would actually deny supplies that could be deemed essential, for which there is no substitute; (ii) notwithstanding the intervention, customary payment would continue to be made to the appropriate recipients; (iii) the development of alternative energy sources would be pursued as rapidly as possible; and, (iv) the intervention would come to an end soon as the oil supplies it makes available can no longer be deemed essential.

In practice, of course, there are all sorts of further difficulties which arise mainly from the fact that those most capable of intervention are also the countries that are least likely to suffer deadly consequences from the denial of Arab oil supplies. Obviously, to remain legally justifiable, an intervention would have to be followed by the establishment of distribution arrangements which would reflect the different intensities of oil-dependence. (Just as in our example, the forcible seizure of the only shop on the island would have to be followed by the equitable distribution of its supplies.) This condition does not, however, raise any great difficulty. The most likely interventionist power, the United States, imports only a fraction of its needs from Arab oil exporters in normal conditions; more generally, the conditions of over-capacity created by the cartel's pricing policy entail the possibility of greatly increasing total availability after an intervention. Specifically, the arithmetic of distribution would have to be worked out in a post-intervention context where some oil previously flowing would probably be cut off (i.e. production from Arab countries which had abstained from the embargo) and where rapidly increasing supplies would be available from the seized oil fields.

In a study entitled 'Oil Fields as Military Objectives' prepared by the Congressional Research Service of the Library of Congress, issued on 21 August 1975, a study whose evident purpose was to depict an intervention as undesirable and unfeasible, the authors cite the UN Charter of Economic Rights and Duties ('no consideration of whatever nature . . . may serve as a justification for aggression') as well as the UN Charter itself, the War Powers Resolution of 1973, and the UN Resolution on Nonintervention, to argue the illegality of an intervention. But in fact, as the authors of the study admit, no conclusive case can be established which would deny the opportunity for illegal justification. Thus, for example, the Economic charter also specifically prohibits the use of economic denial for coercive purposes (ch. IV, Art. 32); and neither does the UN Charter preclude intervention if self-preservation is at stake (hence the legal importance of distribution arrangements that would provide oil supplies to countries where these would avert life-threatening shortages). As for the War Powers Act of 1973 (to turn to municipal law), it merely defines notification requirements, and affirms the need for explicit Congressional approval within sixty days of an act of war. Thus, in spite of their evident desire to make a decisive finding against intervention, the authors of the study were forced to conclude '. . . [that] the legal implications of any U.S. determination to violate the sovereignty of foreign states in response to economic injuries are inconclusive' (page 9). And so they are leaving us not in a vacuum, but rather with the calculus of suffering which is so decisive.

Feasibility

It is understood that the only sensible objective of an embargo-breaking intervention would be the oil-producing region of eastern Arabia, a coastal strip roughly three-hundred miles long from Kuwait to Oman and less than a hundred miles deep at the maximum (Ghawar). That is the total extent of territory which would have to be cleared of any active opposition; the combined extent of the areas which would actually have to be secured on a long-term basis would, of course, be much smaller—being defined by the actual dimensions of the oil fields and their associated facilities, including the major oil-loading terminals.

A crucial aspect of the problem is the Soviet reaction to an intervention. If one takes the view that the Soviet Union would react very energetically, notwithstanding its record in such matters, its lack of direct geographic access (unless Iran were to have fallen under Soviet control in the interim), and notwithstanding also its poor or non-existent relations with the affected states, it is possible to argue that a Western intervention would be a very dangerous affair. The notion that the Soviet Union would actually attack Western forces as they went about their seize-and-hold operation cannot, however, be deemed credible in any circumstances: for a superpower to attack the forces of another (risking nuclear escalation) in response to the latter's operations against third parties which are in no sense allies is simply unimaginable. Other, and much more likely, Soviet reactions might include verbal denunciations and other forms of Soviet political exploitation of the event, threatening military manœuvres, and so on. Such reactions would increase tensions and evoke Western anxieties but would have no practical effect on the outcome. Similarly, it is possible to imagine that the armed forces of the affected states (Saudi Arabia, Kuwait, United Arab Emirates, and so on) would fight valiantly and well, with all the mass of highly advanced equipment that has lately been sold to them. If so, one may envisage prolonged and costly fighting in which heavy casualties would be sustained and much would be destroyed. But again, none of this is realistic. By and large, the local armed forces are incapable of operating their more advanced and powerful weapons without the day-to-day assistance of technicians who are mostly American and virtually all Western. Moreover, even when they can operate their military equipment in a technical sense, its tactical utilization is likely to be ineffectual or nearly so. The simple truth is that none of the states of the area have competent armed forces, for reasons so fundamental that they provide a virtual guarantee of immunity for an intervention force.

Finally, it may be argued that an intervention would ultimately be made futile by sabotage accomplished by local (or imported) guerrillas. If one examines the physical facilities involved, which include hundreds of scattered 'Christmas Trees' at individual well-heads, almost two thousand miles of collection pipes, and the great terminal loading facilities as well as the complex separation, regeneration, and refining plants, one may easily conclude that sabotage would be highly effective in perpetuating the denial of oil following an intervention.

There is, of course, no doubt that an intervention conducted in the 1956 'Hamilcar'/'Musketeer' style, whereby a great sea-borne armada slowly gathered to attack the Suez Canal area, would afford ample opportunity for systematic pre-intervention sabotage. With weeks to do the job, and truck loads of high explosives, it would no doubt be easy to destroy so much that the facilities would in fact have to be rebuilt *ex novo*; and if so, it could take as long as two years to restore full capacity.

But of course the Anglo-French invasion attempt of 1956 is a textbook case of error. Any competently planned intervention would preserve surprise till the end by masking and deception, thereafter inaugurating the proceedings with a sudden descent in commando style at very many separate locations. There are, as it happens, several dozen airstrips fit for heavy transports in the area, and few of them would need to be secured by preliminary parachute assault.

In view of the absence of serious local forces, there would be no need to prejudice surprise by attempting to send in right from the start a large multidivisional force, complete with heavy weapons. Reinforcements and logistic-support forces would of course be eventually needed, but the latter could be provided in a distinct second phase in which it would no longer be necessary to accept preparation penalties for the sake of surprise. As for the initial wave, that should consist of lightly armed élite troops contributed by the participating nations in a combined force which could be accommodated in a manageable number of heavy transport aircraft along with the few small helicopters and light vehicles actually needed right from the start.

In the context of a competent surprise intervention there would be scarcely any opportunity for preventive sabotage, and none at all for systematic destruction. The problem of post-intervention sabotage does, however, remain. Again, it is possible to make an extremely pessimistic estimate on the assumption that oil workers would fight devotedly for the property rights of the local rulers, or the further assumption that they would not be replaced or restricted to non-critical areas; such an estimate is also possible on assuming a major and sucessful effort by local and imported guerrillas. But again there is little substance to such fears. In the first place, the number of oil workers actually needed to *work* the oil fields (as opposed to the far greater number that are kept on the payroll for training purposes or social reasons) is surprisingly small, and does not exceed a few thousand in all. Far from being participating members of the ruling élites, most oil workers who actually work are foreigners, and those who are not Western are kept in a humiliating non-citizen status, which is seemingly deeply resented. Moreover, it would be perfectly possible to replace the totality of the work-force (and operating management) with imported personnel recruited for the purpose. Oil workers are exceptionally mobile, they are used to working in unusual and even dangerous circumstances (at suitable wages) and most of the skilled oil workers all over the world are Americans.

As for the guerrilla threat, it is understandable that the Vietnam-shocked (such as the authors of the Congressional study cited above) should believe that guerrillas are inherently formidable, no matter what the terrain or the human circumstances. In the new post-Vietnam mythology, it seems that the mere possession of a supply of Che Guevara posters, obligatory AK-47 assault rifles, and other such accessories will *ipso facto* create a guerrilla force against which regular forces—and especially those of the United States—must be powerless. Vietnam was full of trees and brave men, and it was a country rather densely populated, in which large bodies of guerrillas could find shelter and food, as well as information and protective masking by implementing Mao's prescription. Eastern Arabia, by contrast, has the totally open terrain of the desert, with a very small population living in settlements extremely well delineated or else easily removable (i.e. bedouin encampments). Moreover, the local population is largely hostile to the rulers (at least in the eastern region of Saudi Arabia) or else indifferent to their interests. In any case, even if the local population were to engage in sabotage or assist outside guerrillas, which is a most unlikely thing, desert conditions will suffice to make such enemies powerless against modern guard forces with night-vision devices, helicopters, and sensor-fences. (It was the Israeli experience that the guerrilla threat was insignificant in the Sinai; and very delicate Negev facilities have been immune from sabotage.)

Nor are the oil facilities as vulnerable as they seem, nor even the pipelines (small-capacity pipe is easily replaced; large-capacity pipe is hard to destroy). There is, above all, the fact that even a great increase in production from present levels would still leave much spare capacity, so that actual loadings would not decline even in the presence of much sabotage.

In the Congressional study cited above, the authors offer a survey of the force requirements they deem necessary for a seizure of the oil fields. Their calculation assumes circumstances described as 'favorable' (page 67) and an intervention limited to the 'Saudi core area' only (defined as the four major onshore oil fields, and their associated facilities). The resulting list of requirements (Table 15, page 69) includes 2 airborne divisions (which require in turn 1,187 heavy-transport sorties), 1 Marine division (in 48 ships), other troops for a total force of 160,000 men, a large number of tactical combat aircraft, 9 air-defence battalions, 16 aircraft carriers, 128 cruisers and destroyers, and an unspecified number of attack submarines. The 'methodology' of the Study is very impressive, and each of its elements is argued with a wealth of detail. If one accepts the results as valid, one is forced to conclude that an intervention—even if limited in scope to the onshore Saudi fields—would in practice be impossible. Apart from the sheer inadequacy of American capabilities (the US Navy only has thirteen carriers, not the sixteen deemed necessary, etc.) there is the very great strategic risk of employing such a large part of the total forces available in one very remote area, thus exposing other sectors (NATO, Korea) to great risk since their reinforcement would no longer be possible. Moreover, the envisaged area of operations does not contain enough export capacity to make the intervention worth while, since the additional output obtainable is inferior to the non-embargo Arab supply likely to be lost following an intervention.

But just as one is on the verge of being persuaded, the exercise is undone by the simple procedure of applying the 'methodology' of the study to military actions of the more or less recent past. And then one discovers that by such calculations D-Day would still be in preparation to allow the accumulation of the requisite number of troops, counted by the tens of millions; that the Falklands operation would have required at least six large carriers instead of two very small ones; that the Israelis would have needed a full airborne division at Entebbe, and so on. In reality, if one envisages a commando action rather than an invasion in the Armada style, the seizure and control of the entire oil-producing region of Eastern Arabia can be considered a manageable military venture (although a risky one) for a Western coalition which would not include American participation. With participation, assuming only competent planning, an intervention should be a relatively straightforward affair which would only entail a very small strategic risk in the form of Soviet counter-intervention, and tactical risks of insignificant proportions.

Desirability

The use of force cannot be desirable; it can only reluctantly be deemed acceptable in circumstances which allow no other choice. It *would* be desirable if oil were afterwards sold at prices which would allow the world economy to recover and resume the progress that the cartel's extortion has interrupted. That desideratum, however, is not to be achieved by force; indeed, it can be said explicitly that a price-motivated intervention would be immoral, illegal, and politically quite unfeasible in any conceivable setting other than those of a denial-price (a price set so high that it would be equivalent to an embargo). In the event of a political embargo, however, force would definitely become a feasible option politically, as it already is militarily; and given the conditions described above, an intervention would also be morally and legally justifiable.

7

Humanitarian Intervention[1]

MICHAEL AKEHURST

In the nineteenth century, there were no rules of international law forbidding a state to ill-treat its own nationals, but other states often claimed a right to use force to prevent such ill-treatment; this right of humanitarian intervention, as it was called, was exercised on a number of occasions by European states, mainly to prevent Turkey ill-treating its Christian subjects.[2] During the present century, and especially since the adoption of the United Nations Charter in 1945, international law has developed a body of rules on human rights, which forbid states to ill-treat individuals, including their own nationals, but at the same time it has developed a body of rules restricting the (previously almost unlimited) right of states to use force. Do the new rules on human rights provide an added justification for retaining the old right of humanitarian intervention? Or do the new rules against the use of force prohibit humanitarian intervention?[3]

State practice since 1945

When the Sixth Committee of the General Assembly was debating the definition of aggression in 1954, the Greek and Netherlands delegates argued in favour of a right of humanitarian intervention in cases where there were ethnic ties between the intervening state and a racial minority suffering persecution in another state. But the Israeli, Chinese, and Panamanian delegates disagreed.[4] In 1947 Yugoslavia sought to justify her support for rebels in Greece by arguing that she 'could not be indifferent' to the persecution by Greece of Slavo-Macedonian minorities, but a Commission of Investigation appointed by the United Nations stated that such persecutions did not absolve Yugoslavia from responsibility for her assistance to the rebels.[5]

On 22 May 1948 Egypt declared that her forces had entered Palestine to protect the lives and property of the Arab

inhabitants of Palestine, for 'Egyptians do not regard Palestine Arabs as strangers since they have been from time
immemorial strongly bound by many ties'.[6] Israel used a
similar argument to justify her use of force to protect Jewish
settlements in parts of Palestine outside the area allotted to
the Jewish State by the General Assembly's partition plan.[7]
But these statements cannot be regarded as true examples of a
state claiming the right to intervene against the wishes of the
local sovereign. Egypt did not recognize the State of Israel,
and regarded the whole of Palestine as rightfully belonging to
the Palestinian Arabs, who had consented to the entry of
Egyptian forces. Similarly, since the establishment of an Arab
state in Palestine, as suggested by the partition plan, never
became a reality, and since none of the neighbouring Arab
states had at that time purported to annex any part of
Palestine, Israel could have argued that her military operations in Palestine in May 1948 were not taking place on
territory under the sovereignty of another state.[8]

Turkey's use of force in Cyprus on behalf of the Turkish
Cypriots must also be distinguished, because Turkey justified
her use of force by reference to the Treaty of Zurich and
did not mention the customary law on humanitarian intervention.[9]

The events in 1971 leading up to the creation of Bangladesh
have been cited by several writers as an archetypal example of
circumstances justifying humanitarian intervention.[10] India's
statements, as reported in the provisional verbatim records of
the Security Council, contain a number of passages justifying
her use of force on this ground.[11] When the final version of the
Official Records was published, however, these statements
had been deleted (presumably by India, since every state is
allowed to edit the record of its representatives' speeches in
United Nations organs); instead, India justified her use of
force by alleging that Pakistan had attacked India first.[12] The
most probable explanation of this discrepancy is that India
had undergone a change of mind and realized that humanitarian intervention was an insufficient justification for the use of
force.

Certainly the reactions of other states provided no support
for the legality of humanitarian intervention. Pakistan, China,

and the United States accused India of aggression and said that India had no right to interfere by force with Pakistan's treatment of the inhabitants of East Pakistan.[13] In the Security Council, Saudi Arabia condemned help given by one state to secessionist movements in another,[14] and Argentina condemned 'secession, subversion and interference in the internal affairs of a State'; Tunisia 'was opposed in any manner to intervention by a third party in the internal affairs of a State'.[15] Most delegates in the General Assembly said that the situation in East Pakistan 'was an internal one, to be settled by the Pakistan government, with no external interference' and expressed support for the principles of territorial integrity and non-interference in the affairs of a member state.[16]

At the beginning of 1979 Vietnam overthrew the Pol Pot regime in Cambodia. But, instead of claiming to have exercised a right of humanitarian intervention, Vietnam denied that its forces had entered Cambodia and said that Pol Pot had been overthrown by the Cambodian people. In the Security Council debate which took place in January 1979, Vietnam's claim that Pol Pot had been overthrown by the Cambodian people (and thus, by implication, not by Vietnam[17]) was repeated by the Soviet Union and its allies (Bulgaria, Cuba, Czechoslovakia, East Germany, Hungary, Mongolia, and Poland). Almost all the other states which spoke in the debate said that Vietnam had acted illegally by intervening in Cambodia's internal affairs. These states included not only Cambodia's ally, China, but also many Western states (Australia, New Zealand, Norway, Portugal, United Kingdom, United States, and, in somewhat vaguer terms, France) and many non-aligned countries (Gabon, Indonesia, Kuwait, Malaysia, Nigeria, Philippines, Singapore, Sudan, and Zambia). Several of these states mentioned the Pol Pot regime's appalling violations of human rights, but nevertheless said that those violations did not entitle Vietnam to overthrow that regime. Not a single state spoke in favour of the existence of a right of humanitarian intervention. A draft resolution, sponsored by Kuwait, Bangladesh, Bolivia, Gabon, Jamaica, Nigeria, and Zambia, which called on 'all foreign forces' (a tactful way of referring to Vietnam) to withdraw from Cambodia and also called on 'the parties concerned' (again, a tactful way of referring to Vietnam) to adhere strictly to the principle of non-interference in the internal affairs of other states, received thirteen votes in favour but was vetoed by the Soviet Union (Czechoslovakia also voted against it).[18]

In November 1979 the General Assembly passed a resolution calling for the immediate withdrawal of all foreign forces from Cambodia, and calling on all states to refrain from interference in the internal affairs of states in South-East Asia. This resolution was, by implication, a clear condemnation of Vietnam's intervention in Cambodia. It is interesting to note that the states voting for the resolution included Greece, the Netherlands, Yugoslavia, and India—states which had previously supported humanitarian intervention. Greece said expressly that Pol Pot's violations of human rights did not justify Vietnam's intervention, and Yugoslavia condemned foreign interference in internal affairs under any pretext whatever.[19]

Three particularly oppressive governments in Africa were also overthrown in 1979, and in each case there were suggestions that a foreign state had helped to overthrow the government in question. But none of the foreign states seems to have invoked the 'right' of humanitarian intervention to justify its actions. French troops overthrew Emperor Bokassa of the Central African Empire, but France tried to pretend that her troops arrived in the Central African Empire, at the request of the *new* government, *after* Bokassa had been overthrown.[20] Similarly, Spain denied complicity in the coup which overthrew President Macias Nguema of Equatorial Guinea.[21] On the other hand, Tanzania admitted that her troops had helped to overthrow President Amin of Uganda, but invoked a different justification for her actions—Tanzanian troops advanced into Uganda to punish Amin for invading Tanzania, and their advance simply happened to coincide with a revolt against Amin inside Uganda. At the summit conference of the Organization of African Unity in July 1979, Sudan criticized Tanzania for invading Uganda and interfering in its internal affairs in violation of the principles of the Organization of African Unity; Nigeria supported Sudan.

President Binaisa, who had been installed as President of Uganda with Tanzania's help, replied that member states of the Organization of African Unity should not 'hide behind the formula of non-intervention when human rights are blatantly violated', which could be interpreted as lending support to the concept of humanitarian intervention, but Tanzania again sought to justify her actions on a different ground, by saying that she had acted in response to President Amin's invasion of Tanzania.[22]

From this brief survey of state practice, it will be seen that the concept of humanitarian intervention has been invoked by states on a surprisingly small number of occasions since 1945, and on each occasion humanitarian intervention has been condemned as illegal by other states. Moreover, the United Nations debates on Cambodia in 1979 provide some evidence that there is now a consensus among states in favour of treating humanitarian intervention as illegal.

The use of force to protect nationals

State practice concerning the use of force by states to protect their nationals abroad throws indirect light on humanitarian intervention.[23] In the nineteenth century European states and the United States often used force to protect their nationals abroad, but it is doubtful whether the right to use force to protect nationals abroad has survived the entry into force of the United Nations Charter.[24]

In 1960,[25] shortly after the Congo became independent, Belgium deployed its troops in the Congo in order to protect Belgian interests and the lives of Belgian and other nationals. In the Security Council debates which followed the Belgian action, Belgium claimed that international law permitted the use of force for such purposes, and the Belgian claim was supported by Italy, the United Kingdom, France, and Argentina; Belgium, Italy, the United Kingdom, and France expressly described the Belgian action as a form of *humanitarian* intervention. The Congo, however, considered that the Belgian action was aggression because it had been carried out without the consent of the Congolese government; this view was supported by Tunisia, the Soviet Union, Poland, and Ecuador.[26]

In 1964 Belgium and the United States sent forces to the Congo to save the lives of hostages of many nationalities (including Belgian, United States, and Congolese nationals) from Congolese rebels. Statements by Belgium and the United States emphasized that the operation had been carried out with the consent of the Congolese government.[27] The reactions of other states varied.

The United Kingdom said that 'under international law a State has a right to land troops in foreign territory to protect its nationals in an emergency if necessary', without mentioning the consent of the local state as a condition precedent for the legality of such action.[28] On the other hand, Nigeria and Bolivia said that the action by Belgium and the United States was lawful only because it had been carried out with the consent of the Congolese government. Brazil and (Nationalist) China also regarded the action as lawful, but emphasized that it had been carried out with the consent of the Congolese government,[29] so it is possible that they, like Nigeria and Bolivia, would have regarded the action as unlawful if the Congolese government had not given its consent.

Of the States which condemned the action, some limited themselves to accusing Belgium and the United States of ulterior motives.[30] The Sudanese representative said:

In normal circumstances it would be difficult to oppose a rescue mission undertaken for humanitarian purposes. But in this particular case . . . the dropping of paratroopers could only have the effect of a provocation to violence.[31]

On the other hand, Ghana and the United Arab Republic condemned the action in terms which implied that a state is never entitled to use force to protect its nationals abroad or for purposes of humanitarian intervention.[32]

The United States intervention in the Dominican Republic in 1965 was defended, in its early stages, on the grounds that it was designed to protect the lives of United States nationals and the nationals of other countries.[33] The United Kingdom supported the claim made by the United States that international law permitted a state to use force to protect its nationals abroad. A rather vague statement by France tended in the same direction, although France expressed doubts about the true purpose of the United States intervention. Most of the states which condemned the action taken by the United States did so for reasons which had nothing to do with the legality or illegality of the use of force to protect nationals abroad, although Jordan expressed doubts about the legality of the use of force for that purpose and one of the statements by Cuba contains a passage which suggests that a state is never entitled to use force for that purpose.[34]

In 1975 the *Mayaguez*, a United States merchant vessel, was seized by Cambodia while she was carrying cargo from Hong Kong to Thailand and was passing close to an island claimed by both Cambodia and South Vietnam. The United States considered that the seizure of the ship was unlawful and used force to secure the release of the ship and of her crew. The United States claimed to be entitled to use force under Article 51 of the Charter,[35] but the action of the United States was condemned as piracy by Thailand and (Communist) China.[36]

In 1976 pro-Palestinian terrorists hijacked a French airliner to Entebbe in Uganda. After a few days the hijackers released some of the passengers, but kept the Jewish passengers (most of whom were Israeli nationals) as hostages, threatening to kill them unless other terrorists, who had been sentenced to terms of imprisonment in several countries, were released. Shortly before the deadline set by the hijackers, Israeli troops landed at Entebbe airport, killed the hijackers, and released the hostages. The Israeli troops also killed some Ugandan soldiers and destroyed some Ugandan military aircraft; Israel sought to justify these actions by alleging that Uganda had helped the hijackers, although Uganda denied these allegations.[37]

The Israeli raid gave rise to a debate in the Security Council. Israel sought to defend her actions by claiming that international law allowed a state to use force to protect its nationals abroad when the local state was unwilling or unable to do so.[38] This view was shared by the United States[39] and (in somewhat vaguer terms) by the United Kingdom.[40] Japan, France, and Italy discussed the legal issue raised by Israel, but without reaching a clear conclusion.[41]

Uganda, Mauritania, Kenya, Qatar, Cameroon, China, Libya, Guinea, Mauritius, Guyana, Benin, Somalia, Yugoslavia, Tanzania, Pakistan, the Soviet Union, Panama, Romania, India, and Cuba accused Israel of committing aggression against Uganda.[42] Uganda, Mauritania, Cameroon, Mauritius, Benin, Pakistan, and the Soviet Union alleged that Israel had used excessive force (for example, by killing Ugandans who were trying to protect the hostages),[43] so it is just possible that they might have accepted the legality of the use of force to protect nationals abroad in other circumstances; but that is unlikely, in view of the hostility shown by Communist and Afro-Asian countries on previous occasions to the use of force to protect nationals abroad. Tanzania and Panama said flatly that a state is not allowed, under the United Nations Charter, to use force to protect its nationals abroad.[44] Guinea said: 'International law condemns the violation of the air space of a sovereign State, unauthorized landing in a country and . . . the destruction of the human and material resources of a State member of the United Nations.'[45] Sweden believed that the Israeli action was technically illegal, but did not want to join in condemning Israel, partly because there was evidence that Uganda had not done as much as it might have done to protect the hostages.[46]

In 1980 United States troops landed in Iran in an unsuccessful attempt to release United States diplomats who were being held as hostages in Iran. President Carter issued a statement in which he described the rescue attempt as 'a humanitarian mission' which had not been 'undertaken with any feeling of hostility towards Iran or its people'; its purpose was 'to safeguard American lives, to protect America's national interest, and to reduce the tensions in the world that have been caused . . . as this crisis has continued'. The United States ambassador to the United Nations forwarded President Carter's statement to the Security Council, 'pursuant to Article 51 of the Charter of the United Nations' (which permits the use of force in self-defence but requires such use of force to be reported to the Security Council); the ambassador also said that the United States had acted 'in exercise of its inherent right of self-defence, with the aim of extricating American nationals who have been and remain the victims of the Iranian armed attack on our Embassy'.[47]

The Security Council did not debate the United States

action, but individual states issued comments on it. Western states tended to be sympathetic towards the United States action, but some other states were critical. Iran condemned it as an act of war. The Soviet news agency, Tass, said it was contrary to international law. So did Saudi Arabia. China said it was a violation of Iran's territorial integrity and sovereignty. Syria condemned it as an act of piracy and aggression. [48]

When the International Court of Justice delivered judgement a month later in the *Case concerning United States Diplomatic and Consular Staff in Tehran*, Judge Morozov (Soviet Union) said that 'Article 51 of the Charter, establishing the right of self-defence, may be invoked only "if an armed attack occurs against a member of the United Nations" . . . [T]here is no evidence that any armed attack had occurred against the United States.'[49] The dissenting opinion of Judge Tarazi (Syria) pointed in the same direction.[50]

The other judges confined themselves to pointing out that the Court had previously ordered the parties not to take any action which might aggravate the tension between them, and that in these circumstances the United States action 'is of a kind calculated to undermine respect for the judicial process in international relations'; they did not deal with the legality of the United States action 'under the Charter of the United Nations and under general international law' because that question had not been submitted to the Court.[51]

The practice concerning the use of force by a state to protect its nationals abroad is relevant, in a number of ways, to any discussion of the legality of humanitarian intervention. On three occasions (in 1960, 1964, and 1980) the use of force by a state to protect its own nationals was described as a form of humanitarian intervention. In 1960, 1964, 1965, and 1976 the individuals protected by the intervention included nationals of other states as well as nationals of the intervening state (but the intervention in the Congo in 1964, which was carried out with the consent of the Congolese government, is apparently the only case in which the rescued individuals included nationals of the local state).

However, the most significant thing about the use of force by a state to protect its nationals abroad is that its legality is challenged by a large number of states. On every occasion since 1960 when a state has used force to protect its nationals abroad, other states have protested that such use of force is illegal. If these protests are well founded, in the sense that the use of force by a state to protect its own nationals is illegal, then it must follow *a fortiori* that humanitarian intervention *stricto sensu* (the use of force by one state to protect the nationals of *another* state against ill treatment by that other state) is also illegal.

Almost all the states which believe that a state is entitled to use force to protect its nationals abroad are Western states. With very few exceptions,[52] other states believe that a state is not entitled to use force for that purpose. Their statements on this issue also enable us to draw inferences about their attitudes to humanitarian intervention *stricto sensu*. For instance, the statements by India and Yugoslavia, during the Security Council debate on the Entebbe raid in 1976, that international law does not permit a state to use force to protect its nationals abroad, suggest that these two countries no longer hold the views which they put forward in 1971 and 1947 respectively in favour of humanitarian intervention; for, if a state's use of force to protect its own nationals is illegal, its use of force to protect non-nationals must be illegal *a fortiori*.

The United Nations Charter

What light do the provisions of the United Nations Charter throw on humanitarian intervention and on the use of force to protect nationals? And what light does the state practice, which has been outlined in this chapter, throw on the interpretation of the relevant provisions of the United Nations Charter?

Article 2(4) of the United Nations Charter requires members of the United Nations to 'refrain in their international relations from the threat or use of force against the territorial integrity or political independence of any State, or in any other manner inconsistent with the purposes of the United Nations'. Some authors interpret Article 2(4) narrowly, arguing that the use of force for a wide variety of purposes (for instance, as a sanction for a breach of international law) is not aimed against the territorial integrity or political independence of any state and is not inconsistent with the purposes of the United Nations;[53] such an interpretation could easily be used to support the view that it is lawful to use force for purposes of humanitarian intervention. For instance, Reisman argues that humanitarian intervention 'seeks neither a territorial change nor a challenge to the political independence of the State involved and is not only not inconsistent with the purposes of the United Nations but is rather in conformity with the most fundamental peremptory norms of the Charter'.[54]

I find such arguments unconvincing. Violations of political independence are not limited to cases where a state is annexed or has a change of government imposed on it by another state, and violations of territorial integrity are not limited to cases where a state is deprived of part of its territory; Lauterpacht argued that the reference to 'territorial integrity' in Article 2(4) meant 'territorial inviolability'.[55] *Any* humanitarian intervention, however limited, constitutes a temporary violation of the target state's political independence and territorial integrity if it is carried out against that state's wishes. (In any case, it is unrealistic to suppose that an entire population can be rescued from really systematic persecution without changing either the government of the persecuting state or the legal status of the territory inhabited by the persecuted population; for instance, how could India have rescued the inhabitants of Bangladesh, except by overthrowing the government of Pakistan or bringing about the secession of Bangladesh from Pakistan?)[56]

It is true that promotion of human rights is one of the purposes of the United Nations listed in Article 1 of the Charter; but so, for instance, is 'international cooperation in solving international problems of an economic, social, cultural or humanitarian character'. Reisman's argument, carried to its logical conclusion, would entitle a state to use force against another state which adopted an uncooperative attitude concerning economic, social, or cultural questions—a startling and unacceptable result.[57] The first purpose listed in Article 1 is the maintenance of international peace, and it is submitted that it is unlawful for states to seek to realize the other purposes of the United Nations by means which involve a breach of international peace; Article 2(4) means that *every* use of force is 'inconsistent with the purposes of the United Nations', unless the State concerned can point to some other provision of the Charter which expressly authorizes the use of force.

Most authors interpret Article 2(4) as imposing a total ban on the use of force in international relations except when another provision of the Charter expressly recognizes or creates an exception to that ban.[58] This broad interpretation of Article 2(4) is confirmed by the *travaux préparatoires* of the Charter,[59] and in recent years has received the support of most of the member states of the United Nations.[60]

Is there any other provision of the United Nations Charter which could be interpreted as authorizing humanitarian intervention by way of an exception to the general prohibition on the use of force in Article 2(4)?

Under Chapter VII of the Charter, the Security Council has a very wide discretion to declare the existence of a threat to the peace and to take military or non-military action to remove that threat. The Security Council could therefore declare that violations of human rights in a particular country constituted a threat to the peace, and could take military action (or authorize member states to take military action) to terminate such violations of human rights. The Security Council has made use of this power once, on a very limited scale, in 1966, when it declared that the situation in Rhodesia (following the unilateral declaration of independence by the white minority regime) constituted a threat to international peace; the Security Council also authorized the United Kingdom to use force to stop ships carrying oil to Rhodesia. Maybe the Security Council ought to make greater use of these powers in future cases. But it must be emphasized that only the Security Council is permitted to act in this way; these powers of the Security Council are not shared by the General Assembly or by regional organizations.[61]

Does Article 51 of the Charter, which permits the use of force in self-defence, provide a justification for humanitarian intervention? The United States claimed that its use of force to rescue United States nationals from Cambodia in 1975, and from Iran in 1980, was justified by Article 51. Some writers regard the use of force to protect nationals abroad as a form of self-defence.[62] Presumably this reasoning could be extended to regard the use of force by State A against State B, in order to protect nationals of State C in State B, as a form of collective self-defence, at least when State C requests the use of force by State A. But it is impossible to invoke collective self-defence to justify the use of force by State A against State B in order to protect the nationals of State B.[63] Thus Article 51 provides no justification for humanitarian intervention *stricto sensu* (the use of force by one state to protect the nationals of another state against ill-treatment by that other state).[64]

Whether Article 51 provides a justification for states using force to protect their own nationals is more controversial. Writers like Bowett, who regard Article 51 as preserving the nineteenth-century law on self-defence,[65] naturally have no difficulty in justifying the use of force to protect nationals abroad as a form of self-defence.[66] Even a narrow interpretation of Article 51, which would allow states to use force in self-defence only after an armed attack has occurred,[67] would not necessarily be fatal to the view that it is lawful to use force to protect nationals abroad, because it could be argued that an armed attack on nationals abroad is equivalent to an armed attack on the state itself, since population is an essential ingredient of statehood.[68] However, most of the authors who adopt a narrow interpretation of Article 51 do not consider that it is lawful to use force to protect nationals abroad; they believe that force may be used in defence of a state's nationals only when they are present on the territory of the national's state.[69] This view was also advocated by Judges Morozov and Tarazi in the *Case concerning United States Diplomatic and Consular Staff in Tehran*, and is implicit in the opinions expressed by almost all non-Western states that the use of force to protect nationals abroad is illegal.

Indeed, there are cogent reasons for interpreting Article 51 restrictively, so as to exclude the use of force for this purpose; Article 51 is an exception to the prohibition of the use of force in Article 2(4), and it is a general principle of interpretation that exceptions to a general rule should be narrowly interpreted in order not to undermine the general rule. Moreover, to equate an attack on nationals abroad with an attack on the national state, as some writers do, is fallacious. Nationals cannot be identified with the national state for all purposes; for instance, a state possesses sovereign immunity in foreign courts, but its nationals do not.[70]

The view that both humanitarian intervention and the use of force to protect nationals abroad are illegal is supported by the General Assembly's declaration of 21 December 1965, which condemns intervention in the widest terms; paragraph 1 declares that 'no State has the right to intervene, directly or indirectly, for any reason whatever, in the internal or external affairs of any other State' and the seventh preambular paragraph states that 'armed intervention is synonymous with aggression'.[71] Paragraph 1 is repeated, almost without alteration, in the General Assembly's Declaration of 24 October 1970 on Principles of International Law concerning Friendly Relations and Cooperation among States, the eighth preambular paragraph of which states that 'the practice of any form of intervention . . . violates the spirit and letter of the Charter'.[72]

It is true that these two declarations do not *specifically* condemn humanitarian intervention or the use of force for the protection of nationals abroad. But they condemn intervention in the most general terms, without mentioning humanitarian intervention or the use of force for the protection of nationals abroad as exceptions to the general prohibition. In the pre-Charter era, humanitarian intervention and the use of force for the protection of nationals abroad were two of the commonest kinds of intervention;[73] if the General Assembly had intended these two kinds of intervention not to be covered by the general prohibition, it would surely have said so expressly.

This opinion is supported by consideration of the antecedents of the declaration of 21 December 1965. Many of its provisions bear a striking resemblance to the Montevideo Convention of 1933 on the Rights and Duties of States, to the Additional Protocol relative to Non-Intervention signed at Buenos Aires in 1936, and to the Charter of the Organization of American States (Articles 15 and 16 of the 1948 version). Nor is this similarity fortuitous; the fifth preambular paragraph 'reaffirm[s] the principle of non-intervention, proclaimed in the Charters of the Organization of American States, the League of Arab States and the Organization of African Unity and affirmed at the conferences held at Montevideo, Buenos Aires, Chapultepec and Bogotá ... '. Prohibitions of intervention in inter-American treaties were deliberately intended to prevent the use of force to protect nationals abroad, which had been frequently practised by the United States against Latin American States before the 1930s. Since the declaration of 21 December 1965 was a conscious restatement of rules laid down in inter-American treaties, it must surely be interpreted in the same way. Moreover, if the use of force to protect nationals is illegal, the use of force to protect non-nationals (humanitarian intervention) must *a fortiori* be illegal.

Humanitarian intervention and the use of force to protect nationals abroad were mentioned by a number of states in the debates which preceded the adoption of the declarations of 21 December 1965 and 24 October 1970. Only a very small number of states claimed that the use of force to protect nationals abroad was lawful, and their views were challenged by a relatively large group of states. A few spoke in favour of humanitarian intervention, and a few spoke against it; the *travaux préparatoires* are thus less illuminating as regards humanitarian intervention than as regards the use of force to protect nationals abroad, but the mere fact that the issue was raised at all indicates that the failure of the declarations to mention humanitarian intervention as an exception to the general prohibition of intervention was not due to an oversight.[74]

General Assembly resolutions are not always of great value as evidence of international law. But the two declarations in question are of greater value than most General Assembly resolutions. They claim to be declaratory of existing law, and they were passed without a dissenting vote. Moreover, they are supported by an important passage in the judgement of the International Court of Justice in the *Corfu Channel* case.

The United Kingdom had carried out a minesweeping operation in Albanian territorial waters, and sought to justify the operation 'as a new and special application of the theory of intervention, by means of which the State intervening would secure possession of evidence in the territory of another State, in order to submit it to an international tribunal and thus facilitate its task'.[75] The Court rejected this argument:

The Court can only regard the alleged right of intervention as the manifestation of a policy of force, such as has, in the past, given rise to most serious abuses and such as cannot, whatever be the present defects in international organization, find a place in international law. Intervention is perhaps still less admissible in the particular form it would take here; for, from the nature of things, it would be reserved for the most powerful States, and might easily lead to perverting the administration of international justice itself.[76]

The United Kingdom also argued that a minefield in an international strait was an international nuisance which any interested state was entitled to remove, by way of self-protection or self-help, if the coastal state refused to do so. The Court rejected this argument also:

Between independent States, respect for territorial sovereignty is an essential foundation of international relations. . . . The action of the British Navy constituted a violation of Albanian sovereignty.[77]

Some commentators have sought to restrict the Court's ruling to the facts of the case,[78] but such attempts are unconvincing. The words 'intervention is perhaps still less admissible in the particular form it would take here' suggest that the condemnation of intervention in the previous sentence was intended to apply to all forms of intervention, or rather to all forms of intervention which involved the use of force ('the manifestation of a policy of force'); the Court condemned intervention in general, and then picked out the type of intervention practised by the United Kingdom for more particular condemnation. Similarly, the Court's statement that 'respect for territorial sovereignty is an essential foundation of international relations' was made without any qualifications or restrictions. It is therefore submitted that the judgement should be interpreted as condemning *all* intervention, self-protection, or self-help involving the use of force— including the use of force to protect nationals abroad or for purposes of humanitarian intervention.

It is often argued that forcible intervention by individual states may sometimes be the only way to prevent one state from ill-treating the nationals of another (or its own nationals), in view of the inability or unwillingness of the United Nations to prevent such ill-treatment. The words 'whatever be the present defects in international organization' suggest that the Court did not have great confidence in the effectiveness of the political organs of the United Nations; yet the Court nevertheless condemned intervention by individual states. It is submitted that the Court's approach was politically sound. Whenever one state uses force against another, there is a risk that innocent people may be killed. The use of force as a sanction for a breach of an international obligation may do more harm than the breach of the international obligation; the cure is often worse than the disease.[79] This is particularly true of the use of force to protect nationals abroad and of humanitarian intervention, which were frequently abused in the past.[80]

A desire to develop more effective sanctions for breaches of international law should not blind us to the possibility that a legal system may be brought into disrepute if sanctions are *too* severe. It is well known that in the early nineteenth century, when a large number of crimes were capital offences in England, juries often refused to convict criminals because they did not want them to be hanged, and such perverse verdicts brought the law as a whole into disrepute. Later in the nineteenth century, European states used force against Latin American states which broke the rules of international law governing the treatment of foreigners, and the excessive means used to enforce those rules discredited the rules themselves in the eyes of Latin American states, which have refused ever since to accept the rules advocated by European states.[81] At present Western states often have difficulty in persuading African and Asian states to accept the idea of a minimum international standard for the treatment of foreigners; if Western states also claim the right to use force as a sanction for breaches of that standard, there is a danger that African and Asian states may react in the same way that Latin American ones reacted a century ago, by rejecting that standard altogether. Similarly, claims by some states that they are entitled to use force to prevent violations of human rights may make other states reluctant to accept legal obligations concerning human rights.[82] What is needed is more effective *international* machinery for the protection of human rights. Humanitarian intervention is an inadequate substitute for such machinery, and may even delay or discourage its establishment.

NOTES

1 Part of this chapter is based on my article, 'The Use of Force to Protect Nationals Abroad', *International Relations*, 5 (1977), pp. 3–23. I am grateful to the editor of *International Relations* for permitting me to reuse much of the material in that article.

2 Ganji, *International Protection of Human Rights* (1962), chapter 1.

3 The following topics will not be covered in the present chapter:
(a) non-military intervention to protect human rights (see Schachter, 'Les aspects juridiques de la politique américaine en matière de droits de l'homme', *Annuaire français de droit international*, 23 (1977), p. 53);
(b) the use of force by a state on territory which it claims as its own (on India's invasion of Goa in 1961, see Akehurst, loc. cit., n. 1 above, p. 5);
(c) the use of force by a state on the territory of another state with the consent of the latter state (for recent examples, see *Keesing's Contemporary Archives*, 1978, pp. 28918–20 (action by West Germany to rescue a Lufthansa airliner, and its passengers and crew, which had been hijacked to Somalia) and 29125–7 (French action to rescue Europeans from Zaire); for earlier examples, see Akehurst, loc. cit. (n. 1) above, pp. 5 and 11–12.

4 GAOR, ninth session, Sixth Committee, 409th meeting, para. 23; 412th meeting, para. 35; 417th meeting, para. 31; 418th meeting, para. 13; *Nederlands Tijdschrift voor Internationaal Recht*, 2 (1955), pp. 167, 176–7.

5 UN document S/360/Rev. 1 (SCOR, 2nd year, special supplement 2, vol. 1, part 3, chapter 1, pp. 109–10).

6 SCOR, 3rd year, 301st meeting, pp. 7–8.

7 Ibid., p. 10.

8 Indeed, the Israeli statement did emphasize 'the absence of any duly constituted authority' in all parts of Palestine outside the area allotted to the Jewish State by the partition plan. Israel also gave an alternative justification for her military operations in those parts of Palestine: her military operations were designed 'to repel aggression and, as part of an essentially defensive plan, to prevent those areas from being used as bases for attacks against the State of Israel' (ibid.).

9 SCOR, 19th year, 1142nd meeting, p. 12; *UN Monthly Chronicle*, August–September 1974, pp. 22, 30.

10 See, for example, *International Commission of Jurists Review*, 8 (1972), pp. 59–62.

11 See the passages cited by Franck and Rodley in *American Journal of International Law*, 67 (1973), pp. 275, 276.

12 See, for example, SCOR, 26th year, 1606th meeting, p. 15.

13 *UN Monthly Chronicle*, January 1972, pp. 5, 7–8, 11; *Keesing's Contemporary Archives*, 1971–2, p. 25069; UN document S/PV. 1611, p. 11.

14 *UN Monthly Chronicle*, January 1972, p. 24.

15 Ibid., pp. 32, 37.

16 Ibid., p. 90. See, especially, the Ghanaian statement cited by Franck and Rodley in the *American Journal of International Law*, 67 (1973), pp. 275, 297.

17 However, in February 1979 Vietnam admitted that it was helping the Cambodian people, at their request, to achieve self-determination against the neo-colonial regime of Pol Pot, 'the product of the hegemonistic and expansionist policy of the Peking authorities' (*UN Chronicle*, March 1979, pp. 13 and 45).

18 *Keesing's Contemporary Archives*, 1979, pp. 29613–21; *UN Chronicle*, February 1979, pp. 5–9; SCOR, 2108th–12th meetings.

19 *UN Chronicle*, January 1980, pp. 39, 41 and 44.

20 *Annuaire français de droit international* 25 (1979), pp. 908–10.

21 *Keesing's Contemporary Archives*, 1979, p. 29885.

22 Ibid., pp. 29669–74 and 29840–1.

23 For discussion of similarities and dissimilarities between humanitarian intervention and the use of force to protect nationals abroad, see Akehurst, loc. cit. (n. 1) above, pp. 13–15.

Help given by foreign states to national liberation movements may appear to be similar to humanitarian intervention, but the similarity is more apparent than real. The idea that it is lawful for foreign states to give help to national liberation movements provides no support for the alleged right of humanitarian intervention, because (i) Western states reject the idea that it is lawful for foreign states to give help to national liberation movements, and (ii) the non-Western states which accept this idea have been careful to confine it to colonial and 'neo-colonial' circumstances, and 'neo-colonial', circumstances seem to be limited to South Africa and Palestine (but cf. n. 17 above). States which advocate the right to use force against colonial or 'neo-colonial' rule have been careful not to present this alleged right as an example of a wider right of humanitarian intervention; on the contrary, those who support the use of force against states guilty of colonial or 'neo-colonial' practices are often the most vehement in condemning any intervention, humanitarian or otherwise, in the affairs of other states.

24 Brownlie, *International Law and the Use of Force by States* (1963), pp. 289–301.

25 For practice between 1945 and 1959, see Akehurst, loc. cit. (n. 1) above, pp. 5–7.

26 *Repertoire of the Practice of the Security Council 1959–1963*, pp. 283–4; Whiteman, *A Digest of International Law*, vol. 5 (1965), p. 522.

27 Whiteman, op. cit. (previous note), pp. 475–6; *American Foreign Policy: Current Documents 1964*, p. 770; UN document S/6063, Annex I.

28 *British Practice in International Law* (1964), pp. 131–2.

29 SCOR, 19th year, 1176th meeting, pp. 4–5; 1183rd meeting, p. 14; 1177th meeting, pp. 19 and 26.

30 See, for instance, the Soviet letter to the President of the Security Council (UN document S/6066).

31 SCOR, 19th year, 1170th meeting, p. 28. But Sudan opposed humanitarian intervention in 1979.

32 SCOR, 19th year, 1170th meeting, p. 23, and 1174th meeting, p. 2.

33 UN document S/6310; SCOR, 1196th meeting, p.14; Whiteman, *A Digest of International Law*, vol. 12 (1971), p. 824; Dupuy, *Annuaire français de droit international*, 11 (1965), pp. 71, 76–7; Geyelin, *Lyndon B. Johnson and the World* (1966), pp. 43, 244–5, 250, 252, and 255.

34 *British Practice in International Law* (1965), p. 13; SCOR, 1198th meeting, p. 13, 24; 1200th meeting, p. 3; 1196th meeting, pp. 26, 29.

35 *American Journal of International Law*, 69 (1975), pp. 875–7.

36 *Keesing's Contemporary Archives* (1975), p. 27239; *The Times*, 16 May 1976, pp. 1 and 6; Paust, 'The Seizure and Recovery of the *Mayaguez*', *Yale Law Journal*, 85 (1976), p. 774.

37 UN document S/PV. 1939, pp. 21, 37, 42–50.

38 S/PV. 1939, pp. 51–5.

39 S/PV. 1941, p. 31.

40 S/PV. 1940, p. 48.

41 S/PV. 1942, pp. 28–30; S/PV. 1943, pp. 28–31 and 36–7.

42 S/PV. 1939, pp. 21, 27, 67, 76, 91–2, 96, 106; S/PV. 1940, pp. 13, 21–31, 36; S/PV. 1941, pp. 4–10, 14–19, 26–7, 42–3, 57–61, 67–72; S/PV. 1942, pp. 13, 21–5, 62; S/PV. 1943, pp. 47–50.

43 S/PV. 1939, pp. 21, 27, 91–2; S/PV. 1940, pp. 21–31; S/PV. 1941, pp. 4–10, 57–61, 67–72.

44 S/PV. 1941, p. 43; S/PV. 1942, p. 17. See also the statement by Guyana, S/PV. 1940, p. 38.

45 S/PV. 1940, p. 16.

46 S/PV. 1940, p. 52. For further discussion of the Entebbe raid, see Akehurst, loc. cit. (n. 1) above, pp. 19–23; Green, 'Rescue at Entebbe—Legal Aspects', *Israel Year Book on Human Rights*, 6 (1976), p. 312, A. E. Evans and J. F. Murphy, *Legal Aspects of International Terrorism* (1978), pp. 554–61.

   A similar attempt by Egypt in 1978 to rescue Egyptian nationals from Cyprus, where they were being held as hostages by Palestinian terrorists, was unsuccessful and was condemned by the government of Cyprus as 'a violation of Cyprus's sovereignty' (*Keesing's Contemporary Archives*, 1978, p. 29305).

47 UN document S/13908.

48 *Keesing's Contemporary Archives*, 1980, pp. 30531 *et seqq.*; *The Times*, 26 Apr. 1980, p. 5; ibid., 28 Apr. 1980, p. 6; *International Herald Tribune*, 26–27 Apr. 1980, p. 2.

49 *I.C.J. Reports*, 1980, pp. 3, 56–7.

50 Ibid., pp. 64–5.

51 Ibid., p. 43. See also Jeffery, 'The American Hostages in Tehran', *International and Comparative Law Quarterly*, 30 (1981), p. 717; and D'Angelo, 'Resort to Force by States to Protect Nationals: The US Rescue Mission to Iran and its Legality under International Law', *Virginia Journal of International Law*, 21 (1981), p. 485.

52 The only *clear* exceptions are Argentina and Israel. But Israel and Argentina do not accept the legality of humanitarian intervention *stricto sensu* (the use of force by a state to protect the nationals of *another* state against ill treatment by that other state). Indeed, the Security Council debates on Cambodia in January 1979 indicate that Western states also have now come to accept that humanitarian intervention *stricto sensu* is forbidden by international law.

53 Notably Julius Stone, *Aggression and World Order* (1963), pp. 43, 95–6.

54 Lillich, ed., *Humanitarian Intervention and the United Nations* (1973), p. 177. See also the chapter by Lillich in J. N. Moore, ed., *Law and Civil War in the Modern World* (1974), pp. 229–51 (but cf. the opposing views of Brownlie, ibid., pp. 217–28); McDougal, Lasswell, and Chen, *Human Rights and World Public Order* (1980), pp. 236–47.

55 Oppenheim, *International Law* (7th edn. by Lauterpacht, 1952), vol. 2, p. 154.

56 When intervention aids a secessionist movement in another state, like the Indian intervention in East Pakistan (Bangladesh) in 1971, it must be regarded as incompatible with the territorial integrity of the latter state on even the narrowest interpretation of Article 2 (4); that was why the United States condemned India's use of force in 1971 (UN document S/PV. 1611, p. 11, quoted in Paxman and Boggs, ed., *The United Nations: A Reassessment* (1973), p. 123).

57 Developing countries often accuse the richer states of adopting an uncooperative attitude towards the demands of the developing countries for the establishment of a new international economic order. Reisman's argument, carried to its logical conclusion, would permit developing countries to use force in order to make the richer states adopt a more co-operative attitude on such economic questions. See also Franck and Rodley, *American Journal of International Law*, 67 (1973), pp. 275, 299–302.

58 See, for instance, Brownlie, *International Law and the Use of Force by States* (1963), pp. 265–8; Wehberg, *Recueil des cours*, 78 (1951), pp. 7, 70 *et seqq.*; Verdross, *Recueil des cours*, 83 (1953), pp. 1, 14; Oppenheim, *International Law* (7th edn. by Lauterpacht, 1952), vol. 2, p. 154; Akehurst, *A Modern Introduction to International Law* (4th edn., 1982), pp. 219–21.

59 The *travaux préparatoires* indicate that the reference to territorial integrity, political independence, and the purposes of the United Nations was added to Article 2 (4), not in order to limit the prohibition on the use of force, but in a clumsy attempt to strengthen it. See the works by Brownlie and Oppenheim cited in the previous note.

60 See the survey by Fonteyne in Lillich, ed., *Humanitarian Intervention and the United Nations* (1973), pp. 209–18; Meeker, *American Journal of International Law*, 57 (1963), pp. 515, 523.

61 Akehurst, *A Modern Introduction to International Law* (4th edn., 1982), pp. 180–4, especially p. 184, n. 1; pp. 186–7 and 226–7.

62 Notably Bowett, *Self-Defence in International Law* (1958), pp. 87–105.

63 It is true that many states believe that it is a lawful form of collective self-defence to assist inhabitants of colonies who are struggling to overthrow colonial rule by force. But this belief is based on the premiss that a colony is a legal entity (a 'self' for the purposes of self-defence and self-determination) separate from the administering power. States which hold this belief have shown no inclination to extend it to contexts which are not colonial or 'neo-colonial'.

64 J. N. Moore, ed., *Law and Civil War in the Modern World* (1974), pp. 44–6. The view that humanitarian intervention is not permitted by Article 51 (or by any other provision of the Charter) is also supported by state practice.

65 Bowett, D. *Self-Defence in International Law* (1958), pp. 184–93.

66 Ibid., pp. 87–105.

67 This is the interpretation supported by most members of the United Nations; see the survey by Fonteyne in Lillich, ed., *Humanitarian Intervention and the United Nations* (1973), pp. 211–13.

68 Bowett, *Self-Defence in International Law* (1958), pp. 91–4. Cf. van Panhuys, *The Rôle of Nationality in International Law* (1959), p. 114.

69 See, for instance, Brownlie, *International Law and the Use of Force by States* (1963), pp. 289–301, especially p. 299; Delivanis, *La légitime défense en droit international public moderne* (1971), pp. 127–8.

70 There may, however, be some exceptions to the general rule that it is unlawful for states to use force to protect their nationals abroad. In particular, a state is allowed to use force to protect its armed forces, even outside its own territory. Article 3 of the definition of aggression adopted by the General Assembly in 1974 provides that aggression includes not only invasion of the territory of another state but also 'an attack by the armed forces of a State on the land, sea or air forces or marine and air fleets of another State' (text in *American Journal of International Law*, 69 (1975), p. 480). The use of force in self-defence against such an attack is obviously lawful (*Corfu Channel* case, *I.C.J. Reports*, 1949, pp. 4, 30–1).

It is possible that merchant ships and civil aircraft are covered by the words 'marine and air fleets' in Article 3 of the definition of aggression; if those words applied only to military aircraft and warships they would be redundant, because they would add nothing to the words 'sea or air forces'. Merchant ships and civil aircraft are equated with the territory of a state for the purposes of claiming jurisdiction over crimes committed on them, and it is submitted that they should also be equated with the territory of a state for the purposes of self-defence. See Akehurst, 'Enforcement Action by Regional Agencies', *British Year Book of International Law*, 42 (1967), pp. 175, 199, and 200, n. 5. Maybe the United States could have argued, as a justification for its attempt to rescue United States diplomats from Iran by force in 1980, that the rule permitting a state to use force to defend its armed forces should be applied by analogy to its diplomatic missions.

71 Text in *Yearbook of the United Nations*, 1965, pp. 94–5.

72 Text in Brownlie, *Basic Documents in International Law* (2nd edn., 1972), pp. 32, 33, 37.

73 The use of force for the protection of nationals abroad was usually classified as intervention, despite an attempt by the United States in 1934 to classify it as interposition, not intervention. The terminology suggested by the United States in 1934 has not been generally accepted. See Waldock, *Recueil des cours*, 81 (1952), pp. 455, 467.

74 See the survey by Fonteyne in Lillich, ed., *Humanitarian Intervention and the United Nations* (1973), pp. 216–17 and pp. 213–18. There was more support for the view that states violating human rights could not shelter behind the non-intervention principle (ibid., pp. 203–9). But the states which took this view usually did not make clear whether they were contemplating intervention by the United Nations or intervention by individual states; and possibly they did not have *armed* intervention in mind when they said that intervention was lawful in such circumstances.

75 *ICJ Reports*, 1949, pp. 4, 34.

76 Ibid., p. 35.

77 Ibid. See also the dissenting opinion of Judge Krylov, who said that [forcible] self-help was prohibited by Article 2 (4) of the United Nations Charter (ibid., p. 77).

78 Fitzmaurice, *British Year Book of International Law*, 27 (1950), pp. 1, 5–6; Bowett, *Self-Defence in International Law* (1958), p. 15.

79 See Franck and Rodley, *American Journal of International Law*, 67 (1973), pp. 275, 300.

80 Between 1815 and 1945 humanitarian intervention was almost never practised unless the intervening state hoped to gain some selfish benefit by intervening; when it did occur, it was usually abused for selfish ends. See Brownlie, *International Law and the Use of Force by States* (1963), pp. 338–42, and Franck and Rodley, loc. cit. (previous note), pp. 277–85 and 290–8.

81 F. S. Dunn, *The Protection of Nationals* (1932).

82 See the observations by Professor Goldman in Lillich, ed., *Humanitarian Intervention and the United Nations* (1973), p. 79. Six years elapsed before the United Nations started to draft treaties to give effect to the Universal Declaration of Human Rights; the drafting took another twelve years; and ten further years elapsed before the two United Nations Covenants on Human Rights received enough ratifications to enter into force in 1976. In thus took twenty-eight years to convert the 'soft law' of the Universal Declaration into the 'hard law' of the Covenants, and at the end of 1981 less than half the states in the world were parties to the Covenants. This illustrates the reluctance of states to accept precise obligations concerning human rights; any suggestion that humanitarian intervention may be practised against states which violate such obligations will inevitably increase their reluctance to accept them.

8
Intervention and National Liberation

RICHARD A. FALK

I

Although the context has changed since the Vietnam era, the interplay between interventionary statecraft and revolutionary warfare is once again at, or close to, the centre of the geopolitical stage. Revolutionary turmoil persists, East–West tensions have heightened, and competing claims by leaders of the superpowers are advanced to justify their armed interventions in other societies to counter the aggressive designs of their global adversary. Political violence is interpreted in relation to global patterns of conflict abstractly associated with such terms as 'global balance', 'strategic interests', and 'world revolutionary process'.

The recent preoccupation with wars of national liberation goes back to the early 1960s when both sides in the cold war fed each other's anxieties. Nikita Khrushchev, in a famous speech on January 6 1961 to a Moscow party congress, emphasized support for wars of national liberation as the main means in the nuclear age for advancing the cause of world Communist revolution. This speech was 'heard' in the West because the United States was also becoming convinced that the critical arena for 'containment' was constituted by the unstable countries of the non-Western world struggling for their independence.

In a sense, Khrushchev's words confirmed John Kennedy's fears. Earlier American strategic doctrine and military capabilities stressed large-scale armed attack across boundaries, more or less along the pattern of the Korean War. But with Castro's 1959 victory in Cuba and the revolutionary struggles beginning to take shape in Indo-China, it became clear to the Kennedy leadership that a different kind of challenge deserved priority in US security planning. Putting the perception most neutrally, it became evident to both main actors on the world stage that the outcome of revolutionary struggles did *appear* to have a direct impact on regional and global power balances. There is a need to stress the word 'appear', as subsequent events would show that a positive revolutionary outcome might not produce the predictable geopolitical effects, as China's revolutionary victory and subsequent anti-Soviet orientation and diplomacy demonstrated rather spectacularly. Manifestly, Soviet security would have been better served by a weak, reactionary China, even if linked to the West, than by a revolutionary China determined to confront the Soviet Union on a variety of ideological and geopolitical issues and make common cause with virtually any Soviet enemy. Nothing has helped the overall international position of the United States in the period since 1945 nearly as much as the victory of China's war of national liberation in 1949.

The basic American geopolitical interpretation of the 1960s acknowledged a 'great revolutionary process' going on in the Third World, to use Walt Rostow's phrase, that the international Communist movement, supposedly directed from Moscow, was seeking to exploit. Rostow's influential formulation defined the essence of the revolutionary process as a struggle against the traditional order on behalf of a commitment to modernization. The Communists enter this struggle, again in Rostow's words, as 'scavengers of modernization', proposing 'techniques of political centralization and dictatorial control' as the basis for rapid economic progress. They seek to gain control over the apparatus of state power in Third World countries by means of guerrilla warfare. The West, according to this view, needs to project a preferred image of modernization, one that combines economic progress with moderate politics, and, in the meantime, protects the society militarily against the predatory effects of Communist-inspired and supported guerrilla warfare. As could have been expected, the military task took precedence and produced an elaborate doctrine and practice of counter-insurgency warfare culminating in years of American involvement in the Vietnam War.

A point worth stressing is the blatantly ahistorical nature of the American contention that this challenge posed by wars of national liberation was something new and frighteningly formidable. This misplaced sense of novelty was ebulliently phrased by Hubert Humphrey, when as Vice-President, he spoke of wars of national liberation '. . . as a bold new form of aggression which could rank in military importance with the discovery of gun powder'. Humphrey could not at the time resist adding coyly that 'it will be recalled that the inventors of gun powder were Chinese'. Underlying this misperception was an accurate realization that these struggles were being determined by social forces that could not be contained or even explained by the standard logic of state power. The only explanation, then, that US policy-makers could come up with was that, as a consequence of Communist perfidy, the weaker side in a military sense seemed somehow to be winning; that is, in a manner ultimately baffling to the militarist mind: 'The people' had been mobilized in such a way as to become a decisive factor.

It was in such a perceptual context that the Vietnam War unfolded. As Dean Rusk, then Secretary of State, put it, 'I would agree with General Giap and other Communists' that Vietnam 'is a test case for "wars of national liberation" '. What Rusk and other American policy-makers meant by a war of national liberation was an essential intermingling of internal 'instability' with *prior* 'vital external support, in organization and direction, in training, in men, in weapons and other supplies'. This vital external support was equated with 'aggression', or at least with 'indirect aggression', as Dulles had characterized Communist influence in the late 1950s. Response by way of military efforts was described by American policy-makers as an exercise of the right of self-defence. The American counter-revolutionary response to liberation struggles around the world became a central issue of international politics, exhibiting a wider American resolve not to appease Communist aggression ('the lesson of Munich').

At the very time that this construction was being put on the character of wars of national liberation by American officials, Communist official thinking, as might be expected, was moving in exactly the opposite direction. Leaders in Moscow and in other Communist countries were telling the leaders of revolutionary movements that they would have diplomatic support and ideological sympathy from the Communist camp, but not material assistance. China in particular preached self-reliance to her Vietnamese comrades, and meant it, as subsequent Vietnamese dismay has shown.

On the battlefield, the United States lost the Vietnamese test case, although why and how remain a subject of intense controversy among American policy-making élites. In the aftermath of Vietnam there was a tactical retreat during the Nixon presidency. *Rapprochement* with China, *détente*, and 'the Vietnam syndrome' combined to achieve a temporary abandonment of American counter-insurgency reflex responses to wars of national liberation. The Nixon Doctrine represented a do-it-yourself injunction to anti-Communist Third World governments, in many ways analogous to the Sino-Soviet stance. The United States would henceforth give sympathy, support, and equipment as needed, but the fighting must be done by the people in the country, except in the case of direct, Korea-style, Communist aggression. This retreat from counter-insurgency activism corresponded to the post-Vietnam mood of the public in the United States on these issues, and it resulted in a fruitful separation of containment thinking from US policy toward the Third World.

Yet the Nixon Doctrine was itself tested by developments in the 1970s, especially by the large-scale dispatch of Cuban troops, with the help of Soviet logistics, to Angola and Ethiopia to consolidate Marxist-Leninist victories, by revolutionary victories in Iran and Nicaragua in 1978, and then by the massive entry of Soviet troops to repress an anti-regime uprising in Afghanistan. These developments were viewed as 'adverse' to the position of the United States in the world and were major ingredients in the recent revival of an avowedly more interventionary approach to political struggles in the Third World, especially those taking place in vital regions of concern such as the Persian Gulf and Central America. The principal American foreign policy question became one of tactical and political preparation—how to achieve an interventionary capability that would be supported by the American electorate and the political process.

II

'National liberation' and 'intervention' are heavily loaded terms, especially 'national liberation'. It is, at once, a juicy centre-piece of East–West propaganda, a principal ingredient of Third World identity, and a fairly accurate way of describing a specific class of armed struggle in the Third World. The main characteristic of this kind of struggle is that its principal goal centres on the elimination of political, economic, social, and cultural structures of domination associated with Western external forces and values. The national liberation framework was initially employed to refer to the anti-colonial struggle by people in the Third World. The West often contended that a war of national liberation was little more than a cover for Soviet-led aggression. The East insisted that the national liberation process involved an internal struggle for full sovereignty against external forces of domination, a struggle whose favourable outcome would strengthen the world socialist position and whose objectives were being resisted, mainly by Western, and then later principally by American intervention.

The Third World's position was oriented around the build-up of the non-aligned movement as an international force that was neither pro-East nor pro-West. Going back to the Bandung Conference of 1955 which deliberately excluded the Soviet Union, the main leaders of the Third World drew a sharp distinction between a global socialist process inspired and guided by the Soviet Union which they reject, and a non-Western movement of solidarity which they try to nourish on the basis of successes in national revolutionary struggles. States like Cuba and Vietnam, because of their dependence on Soviet support, blur this distinction, making it appear that 'non-alignment' is pro-Soviet and anti-American in its nature and that the non-alignment movement is split between an anti-imperial posture and an anti-United States posture. To the extent that national liberation moves in an anti-imperial direction it emphasizes the North–South axis of conflict, while to the extent that it takes on a Marxist-Leninist, anti-capitalist character, it emphasizes the East–West axis of conflict.

Eastern and Third World views correspond more closely to reality than does the Western view, although specific cases express this correspondence in varying degrees. The sardonic Eastern European street joke that 'in Capitalism man exploits man, while in Communism it is the other way around' doesn't apply, in my judgement, to wars of national liberation. There is a powerful historical tendency in the Third World toward national revolution that centres on struggles against various forms of actual Western domination. The Soviet Union does generally support such struggles and often gains from their outcomes, but this need not be necessarily so. Indeed, the greatest Soviet set-back in geopolitics since the Russian Revolution, as already suggested, came from the 'victory' of China's war of national liberation, an outcome that was at the time treated as a major 'defeat' for the West.

The Iranian Revolution is also bewildering if it is seen primarily in these globalist terms. It was a national revolution against Western domination which seems to constitute a set-back for both Soviet and American geopolitical interests, although a more direct one for the United States, but possibly a more permanent and threatening one for the Soviet Union. The dynamics of national revolution in the Third World may correlate, imperfectly, with some parallel dynamics of the East–West geopolitical encounter. The more fundamental point, however, is that although such global connections sometimes exist, the core of such struggles lies between the domestic population of a country and its beleaguered but generally highly armed and often brutal élite. Some Soviet involvement may be present, but it is generally marginal to the outcome, at least until the stage when there has been a heavy involvement by the United States on the other side; it is reactive and defensive, and grows only as the scale of intervention grows.

The anti-Western outcome of several specific national struggles in the Third World, and allegedly insufficient defence spending, fostered an overall impression in the United States in the late 1970s that there was a serious 'decline' in the American world position. The 1980 election of Ronald Reagan as President has certainly been interpreted by his supporters as a mandate to reverse this 'decline', partly by vastly increasing the military budget, partly by taking a more active stance in the face of continuing wars of national liberation, and partly by promoting a more assertive diplomacy *vis-à-vis* the Soviet Union.

Thus the controversy over the civil war in El Salvador can best be understood as the latest chapter in the continuing struggle between wars of national liberation and United States foreign policy. From the Communist side, the conflict has been presented as one more battle by progressive forces to seize power from an exploitative collaboration between domestic élites and imperial centres of foreign capital, a collaboration that has reduced the Salvadorean people over a period of many decades to circumstances of grinding poverty and cultural humiliation. On the American side, the conflict in El Salvador has been presented mainly as a vehicle for Cuban, Nicaraguan, and Soviet expansionism, an outside stimulation of popular discontent in which democratic forces of moderation are trying to avoid the twin evils of the extreme right and the extreme left. The role of the United States, according to this interpretation, is to provide the material help and political support which the 'moderate' government requires to triumph over a mixture of foreign aggression and domestic extremism.

Both sides of this argument reject the accusation of intervention. The Communist side acknowledges no more than a legitimate support for a just struggle by the Salvadorean people, fighting against great odds a cruel enemy that is propped up by American intervention in the form of guns, dollars, and diplomatic pressures. The United States Government claims it is legitimately helping a government whose stability has been subverted by the intervention of foreign powers, although it also acknowledges a set of wider strategic interests to make the stakes of the interventionary game seem high enough. This response by American leaders reflects their particular traditional orientation toward interventionary tactics and their styles of public justification for them. There are some striking continuities in this orientation over a period of time. For instance, there is the American penchant for the imagery of dominoes. Thomas Enders, Assistant Secretary of State for Inter-American Affairs in the Reagan administration, and a veteran counter-insurgency diplomat who pushed hard on behalf of militarist tactics during an earlier tour of duty in Cambodia, offers this characteristic image:

If, after Nicaragua, El Salvador is captured by a violent minority, what state in Central America will be able to resist? How long would it be before major strategic U.S. interests—the canal, sea lanes, oil supplies—were at risk?[1]

Note here the pressure to distort normatively the reality of this national revolution. Mr Enders speaks of 'a violent minority' capturing control, but the phrasing inverts the reality. It is a violent minority in Nicaragua and El Salvador which is trying to retain control by relying on a superior technology of violence to counter and defeat the mobilized demands of the discontented for a new social and political order. As usual in such struggles, the majority, in a polling sense, is probably on or near the sidelines, seeking above all to cope, or in certain circumstances, merely to survive.

President Reagan, addressing the OAS on February 25 1982, expressed most obscurely the issues at stake. He explained American policies in Central America as opposition to 'A new kind of colonialism [that] stalks the world today and threatens our independence. It is brutal and totalitarian; it is not of our hemisphere, but it threatens our hemisphere, and has established footholds on American soil for the expansion of its colonialist ambitions'. In other words, to get around the Latin American anxiety about intervention, Reagan tries to present the United States under the banner of 'anti-colonialism', implying by means of vague overtones of Monroe Doctrine, conceptions of hemispheric defence and solidarity. Reagan casts the external supporters of the Salvadorean national revolution as 'new colonialists' marching to foreign melodies, 'so-called wars of national liberation'. The essence of this propaganda effort, of course, is to put the American role in a favourable normative light—as a defensive undertaking prompted by a concern for democracy and self-determination, although admittedly backed up by US strategic concerns and geopolitical self-interest.

The crucial fallacy of the official American position is the pretence that the external links of the Salvadorean revolution define its essential character. These links are in fact both superficial and secondary, and their magnitude remains largely unsubstantiated. The allegations, however, are indispensable to the overall dynamics of the struggle. If neither side in El Salvador had any outside links, is there any doubt who would win?

In a more fundamental sense the interplay between intervention and national liberation is as old as the state system. There has been all along a continuous series of encounters between forces of domination associated with the interventionary policies of strong states and the liberationist forces associated with the drive for national autonomy by weak states and repressed societies. The structural quality of this struggle in the present period involves a strengthening of the non-Western forces of autonomy or national liberation in relation to the interventionary capabilities of the Western dominant states. One connected but confusing element in this historical context is the consistent Soviet position of hegemony in relation to forces of national revolution, especially in Eastern Europe but also in regard to the colonized nationalities internal to the Soviet Union itself, and, most recently, in such Third World countries as Afghanistan and Ethiopia. Because of the propagandistic dimension of East–West statecraft neither superpower feels inclined to refer to *these* struggles under the rubric of national liberation. To the ideologues in Moscow these struggles are nothing more than American-inspired uprisings designed to destroy socialism; to Washington they are domestic expressions of legitimate discontent about Soviet domination. In this group of conflicts, it is Washington that has the far better and the more persuasive side of the argument. Here, however, historical forces are not as clearly favourable to national revolution by these anti-Soviet movements, with the exception of those located in the Third World. In the First World the Soviet Union has exhibited a massively sufficient interventionary capability in order to maintain its hegemonic position in the face of widely popular national revolutionary challenges, although for a time in 1980 the strength of the Solidarity movement in Poland provoked an apparent crisis in Soviet imperial tactics.

Part of the complexity and confusion attending this issue

arises from certain historical shifts in the normative framework of international relations. Before 1950 or thereabouts, the main patterns of imperial domination in the Third World enjoyed a certain political legitimacy. Colonial title took precedence over sovereign national rights and made recourse to force by a hegemonic actor more of an occasion of enforcement than an instance of illegal intervention. In the Western hemisphere, the United States' hegemonic position was more or less legitimized, or at least accorded early tacit endorsement, by international acceptance of the Monroe Doctrine and its associated practices. Even the League of Nations, despite a certain ambivalence toward the colonial order as expressed through the Mandates System, continued to reflect the world view of the hegemonic actors of the day. The United States' absence from the League undoubtedly accentuated this normative acceptance. The United States has always been difficult to classify in relation to the prevailing normative framework, being an anti-colonial, yet also an imperial actor. From the time of its anti-colonial origins, the United States has traditionally acted as something of a force of opposition to the European colonial system, while at the same time securing its own so-called regional 'empire of liberty'. This contradictory role of the United States anticipates in interesting respects the current contradictory role of the Soviet Union in the contemporary version of this problem.

The rise to geopolitical pre-eminence of two anti-colonial states, the United States and the Soviet Union, has helped to reshape the normative framework of international society. This reshaping occurred despite the fact that American 'anti-colonialism' became increasingly nominal as its preoccupation with anti-Communism took precedence over other foreign policy issues and led the United States to support the colonialist side in a series of critical revolutionary encounters in the Third World. Furthermore, we can identify several elements of this new emergent normative order which reflect the Communist and Third World view that national wars of liberation are 'just wars' deserving support. The West has reluctantly gone along with this underlying view, although it has refused to endorse the specific rhetoric of 'national

liberation' because of its allegedly partisan ideological overtones.

To get the flavour of this overall assault on the legitimacy of
hegemonic rule in the Third World, it is worth noting the
phraseology of several unanimous United Nations declarations and resolutions. These acts are not binding on their own,
but they disclose an altered normative environment which
became established in the late 1950s. For instance, the United
Nations General Assembly Declaration on the Granting of
Independence to Colonial Countries and Peoples of .1960:

1. The subjection of peoples to alien subjugation, domination and
   exploitation constitutes a denial of fundamental human rights, is
   contrary to the Charter of the United Nations ...

2. All peoples have the right to self-determination; by virtue of that right
   they freely determine their political status and freely pursue their
   economic, social and cultural development.

4. All armed action or repressive measures of all kinds directed against
   dependent peoples shall cease in order to enable them to exercise
   peacefully and freely their right to complete independence.[2]

The normative emphasis here is upon the equal rights of all
peoples to autonomy within the boundaries of any particular
state. The frequent reiteration of these conceptions in the
language of the self-determination of peoples and the ubiquitous emphasis on non-intervention in a state's internal
affairs further illustrate this international normative consensus. This consensus on decolonialization does not extend the
right of self-determination to subject 'nations' or 'minorities'
within an established state; on the contrary, the formulations
on self-determination were carefully drafted to exclude threats
to 'national unity and territorial integrity', such as those
posed by internal secessionist tendencies.

This normative understanding was particularly embodied
in Article 7 of the negotiated formal definition of aggression,
which subordinated prohibitions on the use of force to 'the
right of [people to] self-determination, freedom and independence', and affirmed the right of peoples struggling toward
these ends, 'particularly peoples under colonial and racist
regimes or other forms of alien domination', 'to seek and

receive support'. In effect, support for anti-colonial, anti-racist, anti-hegemonic action was legitimated as an exception to the rules on non-intervention. Soviet doctrine and practice have shown very explicitly that since the 1970s the national liberation movement has entered a new post-colonial phase in the struggle of peoples for self-determination and national independence. In the mid-1970s an emphasis on overcoming economic hegemony supplanted the earlier emphasis on the struggle against colonialism. The normative manifestation of this development involved demands for 'a new international economic order'. With the persistence of global economic recession, discord has surfaced, and there is less focus achieved by Third World or Communist claimants for revolutionary transformation of the world economic and political system.

The main significance of this normative development was rhetorical, but not entirely so. The political force of these norms has been greatly diminished by the fact that many Third World governments are dependent in various ways on external support, especially Western support. At the same time, the strength of the national revolutionary ethos has led leaders of such countries to disguise their dependence for fear of compromising their legitimacy. Such tensions between appearance and reality place a premium on indirect intervention of all forms, from the 'covert operations' of intelligence organizations to the efforts of international financial institutions to prop up and shape Third World economies which are closely tied to Western hegemony. This pressure for indirectness and for a covertness of intervention also arises from the nature of domestic public opinion in the democracies, especially in the United States. Because the democratic public upholds values associated with self-determination, and also because it stands largely opposed to the tactics, costs, and negative experiences of previous large-scale overt interventions, it has become increasingly more difficult, even on cold war grounds, to mobilize domestic support for ideologically justified military interventions against national revolutions in the Third World. The current anti-interventionary mood in the United States, however, is neither very deep nor very consistent. It would be misleading to generalize too far from popular resistance to the Carter/Reagan Central American policy. There seems, for instance, to be a general acceptance of the need to defend Western hegemonic interests in the oil-producing regions of the Middle East against 'a second Iran'. There is virtually unanimous public support for the creation of a Rapid Deployment Force (RDF) to be entrusted, as necessary, with interventionary missions that are not even to be rhetorically reconciled with the international normative framework of self-determination and non-intervention, or with UN Charter prohibitions on non-defensive uses of force.

What is particularly troublesome for the future is the danger that these interventionary pressures could become linked to a cycle of escalation culminating in general war. The Cuban missile crisis of 1962 and the nuclear alert issued in the course of the 1973 Middle East War both illustrate the rapidity with which 'local' and 'regional' issues can be globalized. In both these instances, the Soviet Union backed down under American escalatory pressure. There are strong reasons to believe that the build-up of Soviet strategic capabilities over the last decade was, in part, a deferred reaction to this display of 'weakness'. Can we be confident in the years ahead, especially if Western interventionary projects go badly, that bluffs of escalation will not be made and called? It seems as if the unstructured ordering mechanisms of the global political system increasingly exhibit a new type of fragility that could produce dangerous encounters during the 1980s.

Let me summarize my argument in the form of some propositions:

the dynamics of national revolution will continue in all regions of the Third World;

the global position and diplomatic predispositions of the United States will generate a series of interventionary undertakings of varying intensity, having as their objective the defeat of national revolutions;

these efforts will be unpopular with the citizens of the United States and with allies if prominent or prolonged, especially if only justified on vague geopolitical grounds;

these efforts may engender popular support in the United States and elsewhere if persuasively related to the control of strategic resources, especially oil;

the Soviet Union may regard its overall geopolitical position as depending upon neutralizing such direct, overt intervention, especially if the interventionary locale is geographically contiguous to Soviet territory—also if Moscow grows more dependent on imported resources, and places an emphasis on maintaining an 'open door' to markets and raw materials;

the defeat of national revolutions by United States military intervention in this contemporary setting may often be impossible to achieve despite great military and fiscal advantages; battlefield frustations are likely to build pressure to escalate either in the direction of the nuclear threshold (neutron bomb) or in the direction of wider, even of general war (alleging and challenging a Soviet role);

the normative framework of international relations is virtually inoperative in relation to the pursuit of strategic interests, beyond mutual restraints of prudence;

the effects of the contemporary cycle of intervention are generally adverse from the perspective of world order: intensified violence and suffering; heightened international tensions and general war risks; denial of sovereign rights; increased nuclear temptation; defiance of the normative framework by leading states encouraging a deteriorating overall pattern of law-observance; strengthened anti-democratic tendencies in intervening states.

In sum, intervention against national liberation movements is itself a normative defeat for broad values associated with a world order based on the ideology of state sovereignty and self-determination. Such a view does not imply that the outcome of a victorious national liberation struggle is necessarily a normative delight. Statist logic is non-interventionary, accepting as its consequence, the ebbs and flows of injustice and brutality often displayed in the course of severe domestic conflict.

Various geopolitical accretions complicate the current standing of world order. The overriding importance of avoiding general war places a premium on containing conflict within clear boundaries. This normative priority further reinforces the argument for a non-interventionary diplomacy. Such considerations also suggest the desirability of acquiescing in interventionary claims carried on within 'spheres of influence'. Here, statist logic is encroached upon by hegemonic ordering patterns. Deferring to such patterns, as when the Soviet Union intervenes in Eastern Europe, does create a normative tension between lending support to domestic political trends which are perceived as favourable, and the prudential importance of preserving minimal stability of superpower relations as the foundation of world peace.

Normative reform will not be brought about in the years ahead by institutional changes at the global level. The most important normative developments will depend on political assessments made *within* leadership circles of intervening states, especially the two superpowers. To the extent that Washington and Moscow perceive intervention as self-destructive or unnecessary, the preferred normative logic of self-determination will dominate. Such perceptions can be facilitated both by the resistance capabilities and reassurances provided by victorious national liberation movements and by the play of forces within the potential intervening country. The loosening of alliances may also inhibit to some extent interventionary undertakings, as has been the case in Central America as a result of the support given to national liberationist tendencies by democratic socialist governments and progressive political parties in Western Europe.

As long as 'imperial' leadership persists in the superpowers, the compulsion to intervene will be strong whenever there is a perception of the loss of 'control' over a foreign country previously perceived as dependent in a political, economic, or ideological sense. There is no likelihood of the displacement of such leadership in either the United States or the Soviet Union, although the difficulty and dangers of unsuccessful interventions may be increasingly inhibiting, while at the same time such actions provoke the apocalyptic imagination through an anticipation of a general war fought with nuclear weapons, a reality seen as spiralling out of intervention and counter-intervention cycles in Third World countries.

NOTES

1 *Pan-American Society*, 13 Jan. 1982, p. 8.
2 GA Res. 1514 (XV).

9

Intervention in the Third World

HEDLEY BULL

We are constantly being told that the countries of Asia, Africa, and Latin America are the objects *par excellence* of external intervention in world politics today. If intervention is dictatorial interference by outside powers in the sphere of jurisdiction of a state or independent political community, and this is inherently something that is done by the strong to the weak, then it does indeed make sense to seek the chief illustrations of it in our times in the relations between the advanced industrial states of Western Europe, North America, the Soviet Union, and Japan, and the states of the so-called Third World. The Leninist or neo-Leninist theory of imperialism or dominance and dependence encourages us not merely to recognize a high incidence of intervention by the advanced capitalist states in the affairs of Third World countries but also to see intervention as systematic or structural in nature, a built-in feature of present arrangements. This theory, or dogmas constructed from it, provides the common ideology of the Third World coalition of states, that is of most of the states in the world.

Yet if we compare intervention by outside powers in Asia, Africa, and Latin America in the years since the Second World War with the pattern of intervention in the inter-war period, or even more if we compare it with the period from the First Opium War (1839–42) to the First World War, then the most striking difference is that it has become immensely more difficult. One has only to state this thesis and various antitheses immediately suggest themselves, and these I shall go on to consider; but this is the underlying truth, the broad direction in which the argument has to be made. The countries of Asia, Africa, and Latin America, vulnerable though they are in many cases to external intervention, locked as they may be in a system of dominance and dependence, are less vulnerable than they were in these earlier periods. What this reflects is a shift that has been taking place in the distribution of power towards them—a shift which may be slight, which is very uneven as between some Third World countries and others, and which still leaves the advanced industrialized states of the West in the leading position, but which is strong enough to make a decisive difference at least to the kind of intervention that can take place.

In 1914 the greater part of what we now call the Third World was enclosed within the frontiers of colonial empires. Within these frontiers, colonial peoples were the objects of intervention—often forcible, direct, and open intervention—which left them without recourse to the outside world because in terms of the prevailing standards of legitimacy it was not intervention but the exercise of domestic authority. It may be argued that even today, looking at these actions in retrospect, we should not regard them as interventionary because the objects at which they were directed were not sovereign states; Professor Moïsi, for example, in his chapter above, says that French military actions in Africa before 1960, when most French African colonies became independent, do not count as intervention. Yet while this is correct in legal terms, it is too limited a view; not only would this perspective be rejected by Third World opinion now, it was also largely rejected by the peoples who were the objects of Western coercion at the time, and to treat the Western legal view of that period as the only way in which we may view the matter today, is unduly constricting.

Elsewhere in Asia and Africa there were states enjoying varying degrees of formal independence, but except in the case of Japan this fell short of full membership of the society of states, which was then conceived of as a club to which non-European political communities could be admitted only as and when they met a standard of civilization laid down by the original European members. Intervention in the affairs of these states that were non-members, quasi-members or probationary members of international society, in Turkey, China, Persia, Siam, Afghanistan, Ethiopia—intervention which was again often forcible, direct, and open—was facilitated by the fact that these states were not regarded as entitled to full rights of sovereignty. Even in the case of the

Latin American states, whose full rights of sovereignty were widely conceded, international law as it was expounded in the West afforded only limited protection to the weak: sovereign states had the prerogatives, for example, of resorting to war irrespective of the cause, of engaging in forcible measures short of war in defence of their rights, of imposing valid treaties under duress—prerogatives which in the nature of things could be exercised only by the strong against the weak. Concepts of equal right in international relations which are today, for all that divides them, common ground in the debate between Western and Third World states—the equal right of Western and non-Western states to sovereignty, of Western and non-Western nations to self-determination, and white and non-white races to equal treatment—had no place in international law and little in the prevailing international morality.

Nor did these conditions favourable to Western intervention in the non-Western world change basically in the inter-war period. It is true that the self-confidence of the European powers was undermined by the Great War; that colonial independence found a new champion in the Soviet Union; that colonial empires came to be challenged by mass nationalist movements; that anti-imperialist congresses took place which were the beginning of the international coalition we now call the Third World; that in Baldwin's India policy, or Roosevelt's Good Neighbour policy, attempts were made to adjust to a weakening of the structure of Western dominance. But this structure was still standing: the inter-war period saw the rejection of the racial equality clause by the Paris Peace Conference; the expansion of the British Empire to its greatest extent; the conquest of Ethiopia by Italy; the achievement of self-government by the white minority in Rhodesia; the Jewish colonization of Palestine; the discussion among European powers of the bartering of colonies as a means of appeasement. The leading great powers of the period were the leading colonial powers, Britain and France. Nor did their principal challengers have any interest in attacking the colonial system; Italy sought only a redistribution of colonies in its own favour, Germany sought only to construct a new kind of colonial system within Europe itself (thus violating a rule of the game), and Japan, while it menaced the European empires in the East, did so only so as to establish an imperial system of its own, conceived in their image.

In the course of the post-1945 period the conditions for external intervention in the Third World have been made more unfavourable by five developments which I shall discuss briefly: the growth in Asia, Africa, and Latin America of the will and capacity to resist intervention; the weakening in the Western world of the will to intervene; the growing power of the Soviet Union; the operation of the more general balance of power in such a way as to strengthen the hand of the intervened against *vis-à-vis* the interveners; and the emergence of a new climate of international legitimacy, unfavourable to intervention, and especially to Western intervention in the Third World.

First, there has been a remarkable growth in Third World countries of the will and capacity to resist intervention. The most basic cause of this development lies in the process, much studied by historians of nationalism but still in important ways mysterious, by which non-Western peoples ceased to be politically passive and inert, and became subjects rather than objects in the world political process. It is not to do with material sources of power, but with a spiritual or moral awakening among these peoples, at first among small groups of the Western-educated, and later expressing itself in mass movements; it is the process that leads from being overawed by Western superiority to recovering belief in one's own powers, from seeing Western dominance as a fact of nature to perceiving it as something that can be changed, from seeing Western rule as the engine of progress to viewing it as an obstacle to progress. It is the change one can see taking place in the mind of Gandhi, for example, who was for many years a passionate admirer of the British Empire and what it stood for in India and Africa, only then to become devoted to its overthrow.

It is possible to dispute how far these anti-imperialist movements were truly nationalist movements, as opposed to merely anti-European or anti-Western movements; how far they were modernizing movements and how far rooted in tradition; whether there was a sharp break between the apparently nationalist and modernizing movements that overthrew European rule in the twentieth century, and the earlier forms of resistance by traditional forces which had opposed the imposition of colonial rule in the first place, or whether—as is implied in the Third World doctrine of resistance to 'permanent aggression'—there was continuity between the one and the other. What I want rather to emphasize is the result of these movements, which was that they captured control of *states*: in some cases old states, like China or Persia or Egypt, in other cases new states, based on the boundaries of the former colonial territories.

States are the great agencies whereby communities can impress themselves on world affairs, and the capture or creation of these hundred or so states provided the basic means whereby Asian and African communities could offer resistance to external intervention. Today it is the thesis both of Leninist or neo-Leninist exponents of 'dependency theory', and of liberal-capitalist exponents of the global power of the multinational corporation, that Third World states are mere superstructures incapable of resisting the economic forces that impinge upon them. This is profoundly mistaken: organized as sovereign states, the peoples of the Third World have been able not merely to assert for themselves the legal right to independence of external control and supremacy over their own territories, but also in substantial degree to achieve these objectives in reality. They have used state power to national-ize foreign property, control external economic relations, curb alien minorities, and promote economic growth. Equipped with the international personality that statehood has confer-red upon them, they have fashioned foreign policies, and used them to diversify their external relations and reduce reliance on former colonial masters, to combine with allies and drive wedges among opponents, and to promote domestic cohesion. They have learnt the importance of collaboration with one another, first in the Afro-Asian movement of the 1950s, then in the non-aligned movement of the 1960s, and in the Group of 77. They have used their numbers in United Nations assemblies to change the international rules of the game profoundly in their favour. They have in some cases acquired substantial military power: China and India have exploded nuclear devices, several have significant arms industries, and very many have the capacity, if not to defeat Western intervention, then at least to ensure that the price for it is unacceptably high. In many of these endeavours the achievements of Third World peoples have fallen far short of their aspirations, but they have nevertheless been sufficient to transform the political structure of the world.

Secondly, there has been a weakening in the Western world of the will to intervene, by comparison with earlier periods, or at least of the will to do so forcibly, directly, and openly. Of course, the Western powers have done a great deal of intervening in Third World countries since 1945—more particularly the Western European states and the United States, who until the 1970s had a monopoly of forcible, direct, and open intervention in these areas. The many Third World states that have been weak, unstable, and riven by internal conflicts and tensions have presented, as Professor Hoffmann notes above, 'targets of opportunity'. The Western powers have not been lacking in motives. Economic motives, especially the protection of investments, have played some part in bringing about French interventions in francophone Africa, British interventions in South-East Asia, and United States interventions in Central America. Ideological motives have also been strong—the waning imperialist ideologies of the European colonial powers, who sought either (as in the case of Portugal until 1974) to maintain their colonial dependencies, or at least to control the pace and direction of decolonization, the waxing (at least until the Johnson administration of 1963–8) libertarian and anti-Communist ideology of the United States. Motives arising out of the pursuit of security and power have been especially compelling for the United States, committed as it has been to a struggle with the other superpower, requiring that intervention be met by counter-intervention in every corner of the globe.

The will of the Western countries to intervene, moreover, has not been uniform throughout the period; there have been ups and downs, and the pattern has varied as between one country and another. In the late 1970s and 1980s, at least in the United States, there has been a revival of belief in intervention, by comparison with the low point it had reached during the years of withdrawal from Vietnam 1969-73, and the two years following it. This revival has been fed by the demand for some response to the rise of Soviet interventionism in Africa and South West Asia, the sense of wounded national pride occasioned by set-backs received at the hands of Third World states (China's entry into the United Nations, the defeat in South-East Asia, the Arab oil embargo, the Tehran hostage crisis), and the new rationale for intervention provided by access to resources.

But the idea that the post-1945 period has been one of increased rather than of reduced Western willingness to intervene forcibly, directly, and openly, is an optical illusion. What has increased is not the incidence or scale of Western interventions, but our awareness of them, our perception of them as interventions, and our disposition to disapprove of them. Acts of coercion which in earlier periods were not viewed as interventionary, at least by the Western powers who engaged in them, have come to be seen as such; the rules of non-intervention have been redrawn in such a way as to encompass acts by Western against non-Western societies that previously escaped the net; these new rules are loudly proclaimed by governments representing the majority of states, violations of them are reported; and a powerful new consensus has taken shape against intervention of the old type, which the Western countries are in no position to disregard.

If we consider the post-war period as a whole, it is clear that in the course of it the will of the Western powers to engage in the older kind of intervention came to be broken: for the British and French, especially at Suez in 1956, for the Americans in Vietnam, for the Portuguese and Spanish only in the 1970s. This does not mean that it cannot be revived again, under the stress of a disintegrating international order, but the record shows not only an appreciation by Western governments of the mounting costs of the gunboat style of intervention, in terms of both domestic and international opprobrium, but also a tendency to question the gains: the maintenance of alien rule over subject peoples, or the conspicuous use of the armed forces of the metropolitan power to support or unseat local governments with no shred of local legitimacy, have come to seem means of promoting one's economic, ideological, or security objectives which are best avoided.

Thirdly, Western intervention has been made more difficult by the growing power of the Soviet Union and its allies. The Soviet Union sees itself, not without cause, as the champion of oppressed Asian, African, and Latin American peoples, and their ally in the struggle against colonialism, neo-colonialism, and white supremacism. The rhetorical or ideological alliance between the Soviet state and anti-imperialist movements has been a feature of the world scene since 1917, and has been a natural alliance of weaker sections of international society against the dominant Western segment, but it has only been in the post-1945 period, and especially in the 1960s, 1970s, and 1980s that the Soviet Union has had been able to deploy sufficient military power in Third World areas to place serious obstacles in the path of Western intervention.

No doubt the Soviet Union has given priority to its own state interests and ideological objectives, and has been opportunistic in its attitude to anti-imperialist and Third World movements, extending support to them and withdrawing it as these prior objectives dictate. No doubt also there have always been inherent obstacles of an ideological nature to full co-operation between Soviet communism and bourgeois nationalist movements, rooted in Marx's own failure to recognize the importance of nationality, and in the primacy given to class struggle over struggles among nations and states. The Soviet doctrine of national liberation, according to which nations are not liberated by the achievement of political independence alone, but only by fundamental economic and social transformation, has always been unacceptable to some elements in Third World countries. It is also true that the Soviet Union is a superpower, a mainly European power, a power whose frontiers were established in the era of European expansion—all of which features make it vulnerable to Third World pressures, which China does its best to exploit: on issues such as unequal treaties, nuclear proliferation, the Law of the Sea conference, reform of the UN Security Council, the Soviet Union is sometimes aligned with Western powers against Third World states. Moreover, as the Soviet Union's own capacity for intervention in the Third World has grown, and has been demonstrated in the Middle East in the 1960s, and in Africa and South West Asia in the 1970s, it has begun to engender some of the same antagonism that previously was directed only at the Western countries—above all in the case of its intervention in Afghanistan, which earned it the condemnation both of the UN General Assembly and of the Islamic Conference.

Nevertheless, the Soviet Union has facilitated Third World resistance to Western intervention, and it has been the latter (expressed in the institutionalized or legitimized intervention of the colonial system, in neo-colonial or post-colonial forms of coercive interference, and in support extended to settler regimes) that the Third World as an international coalition has been chiefly concerned to resist. Except in Asia, where its own position is very vulnerable to the same forces that have worked to undermine Western positions in other parts of the Third World, the Soviet Union had the good fortune not to inherit the colonial or quasi-colonial positions that have made the Western countries targets of resistance; its interventions in Africa, unlike some of those of Britain, France, Belgium, or Portugal, have been consistent with the consensus of the Organization of African Unity: even in the Angolan civil war, (where admittedly there was no OAU consensus as to which of the contending factions was the legitimate government until South African intervention brought this into being) and in Ethiopia, this has been so. The great weakness of the Soviet Union in the Third World has been its inability to extend economic and technical assistance on the scale of the Western powers. But by maintaining pressure on the Western powers in Europe and East Asia, by developing its strategic nuclear forces to the level where they began to match those of the United States, by its arms transfers to Third World governments and national liberation movements, and by depriving the West of its monopoly of global naval and interventionary power, it greatly qualified the dominant position which the Western countries had previously enjoyed in the Third World, and eased the task of those working to undermine it.

For twenty years after the end of the Second World War the United States Navy had a position of such assured command of the sea that it was mainly devoted not to defending this position against others but to what was called 'the projection of power ashore'. The expansion of Soviet naval power has brought this to an end. It has never seemed likely that the Soviet Union will replace the United States as the leading naval power, but it has brought about a position where, in place of the dominance of the oceans by one superpower and its lesser naval allies, there is a closer approximation of equilibrium. In this respect the growth of Soviet naval power over the last twenty years may be compared with the growth of German naval power 1898–1914, which qualified British naval supremacy in a comparable way, and led to vast changes in the political structure of the world. If we contemplate this new factor of equilibrium between the superpowers in the Third World from a narrowly Western perspective, it must appear as an unwelcome development; it would be a mistake, however, to assume that it is generally unwelcome in the Third World.

This brings me to the fourth development that has inhibited the older kind of Western intervention: the emergence of a global equilibrium of power unfavourable to intervention—an equilibrium to which the rise of Soviet power has contributed, but of which it is only part. Since the 1950s the Third World has provided the great zone of competition between the Western powers and the Soviet Union, a fluid area of more or less open struggle, by contrast with the northern, industrialized world, where the lines are firmly drawn. Out of this struggle there has emerged a balance among the interveners which has worked to the advantage of the intervened against.

It is true, of course, that it is this global struggle for power that supplies much of the motivation for external intervention and counter-intervention in the Third World. The Western powers and the Soviet bloc, moreover, conduct their competition according to certain tacit rules, which make intervention in Third World areas more feasible than within one another's primary spheres of influence, in Europe; peace between the superpowers and their NATO and Warsaw Pact allies has been preserved, where war and the possibility of war, in much of Asia, Africa, and Latin America, are the norm. This idea of a distinction between a European area, in which peace should be maintained, and an extra-European area in which war may take place without endangering the peace of Europe, may be traced to the origins of the modern states-system; it appears at the time of the Treaty of Cateau-Cambrésis of 1559 between France and Spain, where a verbal agreement allowed that beyond a line west of the meridian of Azores and south of the Tropic of Cancer, violence need be no breach of the Treaty, and ships captured were good prizes; this conception of the division of the world by the 'amity lines', the understanding that there was 'no peace beyond the line', became a rule of customary international law; it appeared in the eighteenth century in the distinction between *paix maritimes* and *paix continentales*; and in the post-colonial period it was revived to become one of the ground rules of the cold war.

But while the world competition for power has provided a motive for outside intervention in this way, and Third World states stand to lose when rules of the competition are drawn up at their expense, they also stand to gain from the competition: so long as the external interveners are divided and no one of them is preponderant, it may be possible to play one off against another. When China's independence was menaced by the United States, as it was for twenty years after the establishment of the People's Republic, the Soviet Union was its guarantor, just as the United States has become China's guarantor now that it is menaced by the Soviet Union. When Egypt's independence was threatened by Britain and France, the United States and the Soviet Union were able to neutralize them. Cuba's survival in the face of United States pressures has depended on its alliance with the Soviet Union, which was able to breach the sphere of American hegemony in the Caribbean. Pakistan's independence of India has depended upon its relations with the United States and later China. Vietnam's ability to withstand intervention by China depends upon its relationship with the Soviet Union, just as Cambodia's prospects of independence of Vietnam are bound up with the assistance it receives from China. There is no need to multiply examples.

I do not suggest that this ability of the potential victims of intervention to maintain themselves by exploiting the divisions among the interveners is peculiar to the post-1945 period. In the era of European expansion a number of states were able to pursue this policy successfully, and owed their survival to it: the ring of buffer states between Great Britain and Russia in Asia, Siam between Britain and France, Ethiopia similarly in Africa, are famous examples. But there were long periods of the domination of particular parts of the extra-European world by a single power: the United States in Central and later South America, after the Civil War; Britain in the Indian Ocean littoral throughout the nineteenth century and much of this century, and in the Middle East in the interwar period; Russia in central Asia. And in the nineteenth century the Concert of Europe, despite some fissures, operated to preserve an element of solidarity among the interveners, as in the partitition of Africa.

The concept of a balance of power or equilibrium, which has played such a large part in the international history of Europe, has never applied to international relations outside Europe; the history of Europe's relation with the rest of the world in the age of its expansion is less one of balance among the contending expanding powers, than it is one of a succession of hegemonies—Spanish or Spanish-Portuguese, Dutch, French, British, and American or Anglo-American; still less has there been any conception, such as that which emerged in Europe, that a balance of world powers is a desirable state of affairs which should be perpetuated —although as Ludwig Dehio points out, the idea that British dominance at sea ought to be resisted for the same reasons as Louis XIV's or Napoleon's dominance on the land was one of the themes of German political thinking in the nineteenth and early twentieth centuries.[1] The breakdown of solidarity among the Western interveners, and the reappearance of conflict and equilibrium, have worked to facilitate Third World resistance to outside intervention.

Fifthly, there has emerged a new climate of international legitimacy unfavourable to intervention, and especially to Western intervention in the countries of the Third World: since 1945, largely although not exclusively because of the dominant influence of Third World countries in the UN system from the 1960s onward, there has been a profound change in our moral and legal notions of the justification of intervention.

The UN Charter, written primarily by the Western powers, its preamble drafted in part by the Prime Minister of South Africa, was basically similar to the Covenant of the League of Nations in the protection it afforded to the old colonial order, with international accountability restricted to Trust Territories and no obligations imposed upon colonial powers to promote self-government in colonial territories. By 1960 the General Assembly had passed the Declaration on the Granting of Independence to Colonial Countries, eliminating the distinction between Trust Territories and other dependent territories for all practical purposes, demanding self-government for all of them, establishing independence as the preferred mode of self-government, and asserting the right of the UN to involve itself in what had previously been regarded as the domestic affairs of the colonial powers. By 1965 it had endorsed the conception of the right of nations to launch wars of national liberation against colonial rule, the right of third parties to intervene on their behalf, and the illegitimacy of the use of force to oppose them. Ten years later it had asserted the right of the UN's own organs to involve themselves in just wars of national liberation, as with SWAPO's campaign in Namibia; it had extended this conception to embrace the cases of Israel and South Africa; and in calling for mandatory sanctions against the latter it was giving effect to Christian Wolff's idea of just intervention endorsed by the *civitas maxima* against a recalcitrant member state.

A full account of the changes that have taken place in the legal and moral climate affecting intervention would have to mention also the obstacles erected in the path of the old prerogative right of states to resort to force; the changes that have taken place in the law of treaties, asserting the invalidity of treaties concluded under duress; the changes in the law with regard to the nationalization of foreign property, and compensation to be paid for it, repudiating 'the international standard' and enabling compensation to be determined by local authorities; and indeed the whole legal and moral assault on behalf of the idea of a New International Economic Order.

Of course, it is necessary to bear in mind that the ideas of the legitimacy of intervention which prevail in the world are broader than one would gather merely from studying the records of the United Nations. Some of the changes I have been describing, especially those carried through in the 1970s and 1980s, have been bitterly opposed by the Western powers. The process by which Third World majorities, sometimes with the assistance of Soviet bloc countries, have captured the political organs of the UN, and used them to change the rules of the game, resulted in the alienation of much Western opinion from a UN system in which the Western powers once occupied the leading position. Indeed, the emergence of the new normative climate in the UN system has been accompanied by a certain weakening of the underlying consensus about the legal rules of international society, disguised by a tendency to substitute 'soft' law for hard law, to rely on rules or principles which cannot be said to have strict legal status. It is only if one takes the view championed by Professor Higgins above, that international law is not a body of rules but a process of authoritative decision that one can avoid coming to the conclusion that a certain deterioration of international law has set in, the ultimate effect of which may be not to inhibit or regulate intervention but to facilitate it. Nevertheless, leaving aside the question of what is law, the changes reflected in the political organs of the UN are an important index of the shift that has taken place in the normative climate of intervention. Historians of decolonization often tell us that UN resolutions have no causal effect because they are ignored or despised by the decision-makers concerned in particular cases. But this is a shallow view: UN resolutions are not something apart from the beliefs and perceptions of those who take decisions in particular countries, but arise out of their processes of political decision, and, once they are formalized and sanctified, are fed back into them, however imperfectly.

For these five reasons, then, intervention of the forcible, direct, and open kind by the Western powers has been rendered more difficult in the decades since the Second World War. It is necessary, however, to consider some antitheses. First, the decline of this kind of intervention on the part of the Western European powers and the United States has been accompanied (and in some measure compensated for) by the rise of new interveners. Not only has the Soviet Union emerged as a practitioner of this kind of intervention, the period has also witnessed the emergence of a number of Third World interveners, some of whom have established local systems of dominance or hegemony. No account of intervention in the post-1945 period would be complete without mention of China's interventions in Korea, Tibet, India, and Vietnam; India's interventions in Kashmir and East Pakistan (the annexation of Goa can hardly be called an intervention, unless we were to take the view that it was an intervention in Portugal); Indonesia's interventions in Malaysia during its policy of confrontation, and in West Irian and East Timor, leading ultimately to the annexation of both territories; Egypt's intervention in the Yemen; Libya's intervention in Chad; Turkey's intervention in Cyprus; Syria's intervention in the Lebanon; Cuba's interventions (although these have been vicarious ones) in Angola and Ethiopia; and Vietnam's interventions in Laos and Cambodia. In calling these uses of force interventions I make no judgement as to whether they were justified or not, but if we are to count Western actions as interventionary on the ground that, whether or not they constituted interference within the jurisdiction of other independent political communities, they were seen as such by some of the parties concerned, then this is the historical criterion we must apply in these cases also.

The crucial question which arises about the new interveners is whether or not the factors that have provided obstacles to the traditional, Western interveners will prove equally inhibiting for them. The political awakening of Third World peoples that brought about the struggle aginst Western colonialism and neo-colonialism, now receding into the past, has also strengthened their capacity to resist intervention by the Soviet Union, or by the stronger states among their own number. The factor of a greater equilibrium of power in Asia, Africa, and Latin America, the possibility which exists of playing off one potential intervener against another, has strengthened Third World countries against the Western powers, and also strengthens them against other interveners. The new legal instrumentalities, abolishing or restricting the old rights to the use of force which the strong once enjoyed against the weak, may be invoked, and have been invoked, by weak Third World countries against the Soviet Union and against strong

Third World countries, just as they have been against the old oppressors, the Western powers.

On the other hand, many of the barriers against intervention which the Third World states have created are the product of a historical movement, gathering a powerful momentum over the last four decades and not yet spent, which has been directed specifically against domination by the Western powers. These barriers do not provide so strong a defence against domination by others. The solidarity that the Third World coalition has maintained so impressively against Western colonialism does not encompass the rule of Han Chinese over Tibetans, Indians over Nagas, Javanese over Melanesians, Iranians and Iraqis over Kurds. The doctrine of a right of nations to wage just wars of liberation may be invoked against alien rule by Western governments, but not to dismember Third World states. There is no consensus against Indian hegemonism in the Indian subcontinent, Vietnamese hegemonism in Indo-China, Libyan hegemonism in North Africa, Nigeria's aspirations to a sphere of influence in West Africa, or Brazil's to one in South America, comparable with the consensus that displayed itself against British hegemonism in the Middle East or United States hegemonism in the Caribbean. The racism displayed by Vietnamese in relation to Chinese, black Africans in relation to East African Asians, Brazilians in relation to Amerindian minorities, will engender opposition within the Third World, but it will not unleash the torrent of protest, to which every stream of opinion throughout Asia and Africa will make its contribution, as racism does when it takes the form of white supremacism. The defences which have been put up against intervention in the Third World have a huge fault running through them; they have been constructed for a particular purpose which has now been achieved in large measure; for other purposes for which in future they will be needed more, they are less than adequate.

A second antithesis which may be stated is that there has been a change in the kind of intervention that has taken place: the Western powers have substituted non-forcible forms of interference for forcible ones, indirect intervention for direct, and clandestine or secret methods of intervention for overt or open ones. It has been pointed out that when Britain became seized by the imperialist fever of the 1880s which led to colonial annexations on a large scale, this had been preceded in the mid-Victorian years by a period of reliance on 'informal empire', the change from the one to the other being one of style and method, not basic principle and purpose.[2] Rather in the same way, it may be argued that as formal empire has receded into the past, 'informal empire' came to the fore once again. Colonial rule, punitive expeditions, and gunboat threats were abandoned because the metropolitan powers sensed that they were no longer effective: IMF credit with strings attached, arms transfers to local proxies, and CIA operations replaced them.

The early 1970s is one period that provides a good deal of evidence that such a change of style and method was taking place. As the United States was withdrawing its armed forces from Vietnam and Great Britain was closing down its garrisons East of Suez, this was rationalized by the argument that forcible means of intervention were no longer the most appropriate ones; there was a great deal of talk, at this time, about 'resources power', and the need to meet 'oil power' with 'food power'; elaborate, academic theories explained how in the new world being created by the growth of 'transnational relations' or 'complex interdependence', force was of declining utility and economic factors were assuming a more central position. Certainly in South-East Asia the absence of the United States and British armed forces that had played such a prominent rôle in the 1960s and earlier, meant that economic levers would assume a greater prominence *faute de mieux*.

At the same time direct means of American and British intervention were giving place to indirect means. The United States, as it withdrew its troops, set about 'the Vietnamization of the war'; the 'Nixon Doctrine', first proclaimed in 1969, required the local allies and associates of the United States to assume the primary part in their own defence, assigning to the United States itself only a back-stop role; the Five Power Agreements, which Britain made for defence co-operation with Malaysia, Singapore, Australia, and New Zealand, so as to offer a substitute for its former military predominance in peninsular South-East Asia, similarly implied a shift of responsibility from metropolitan to local hands. The United

States at this time developed the idea that Western interests in the Gulf region, after Britain's withdrawal, would rely upon the 'twin pillars' of Iran and Saudi Arabia; these and other countries that were inheriting the positions being vacated by the Western great powers—Nigeria, Brazil, Indonesia, sometimes India, Japan, Australia, the so-called 'regional hegemones' (a later term for them, coined by Dr Brzezinski, was 'the new influentials') came to be viewed (perhaps unrealistically) as the local agents, or potential local agents, of Western policies. A shift was taking place also at this time from overt to more covert forms of intervention; this was the period of intensified 'secret bombings' carried out by the United States in Cambodia.

The crucial question that arises about this second antithesis is whether the newer forms of intervention were really an effective substitute for the old ones. No doubt it may be argued that the change of means did enable the intervening Western powers to disengage from methods of intervention that were proving too costly in terms of international and domestic opprobrium, while also salvaging something of their former power or influence in the areas concerned. No doubt the changes represented, from the point of view of the Western states concerned, intelligent adjustments to the changed character of the international system. But it would not be true to say that the new methods left the interveners in as dominant a position as they had been before, when the old methods could still be used effectively. Economic incentives and pressures may be a good substitute for military coercion when the latter is not available, but it does not bring with it the physical control over a people which is willing to forgo the incentives and resist the pressures. Indirect intervention has the disadvantage, compared with direct intervention, that the intervener does not control his local proxy states or agents in the way he controls his own armed forces: the regional 'pillars' may crumble, or pursue policies of their own. Secret or clandestine intervention is usually limited in scale; moreover, in Western democracies at least, it does not long remain secret. At all events, it is clear that the new methods tried in the 1970s did not enable the United States and Britain to retain the position they once occupied in South-East Asia.

A third and final antithesis is that intervention has become more, not less pronounced in the post-1945 world because the development of the world economy, and along with it the deepening contrast between the rich and strong states of the so-called north and the poor and weak states of the south, have made it endemic; in a way that it was not before, intervention has become part of the very structure of the international system itself.

This is not the place for a full consideration of the body of ideas that go by the name of 'dependency theory' or 'the structuralist approach to international relations' but I can indicate briefly what I believe to be its strengths and weaknesses in the present connection. It is true, of course, that the development of the international economy was in no way interrupted by the demise of the colonial system and of the older forms of Western intervention. Nor did it interrupt the growing involvement of Third World countries in the international economy: for most of them links of trade and investment with the outside world have a far deeper impact on their economies today than they did in the colonial era, and on their societies and political systems also. There is many a corner of the Third World which in colonial times was scarcely touched by the European authority to which it was nominally subject, but which today for better or worse bears all the marks of modernity.

It is obvious also that the position occupied by Third World countries in the world economy, although to different degrees and with important exceptions, is one which makes them very much more vulnerable to decisions taken in the Western countries, than the latter are vulnerable to decisions taken in the Third World. Because the term 'interdependence' is often taken to suggest a kind of vulnerability to decisions taken in other countries that is mutual, or perhaps even equal or comparable, the relations between the Western countries and most of the countries of Asia, Africa, and Latin America are indeed better described in terms of dominance and dependence. This relationship of one-sided dependence helps to sustain the conditions in which intervention in the affairs of Third World countries is an option for Western governments.

It is not the case, however, that this inequality of wealth

and power is itself an intervention in the affairs of the poorer and weaker countries. No doubt the inequality between the Western and Third World countries is undesirable; for reasons both moral and practical, which do not need to be elaborated here, we should work for a world in which wealth and power are less unevenly distributed. But if we are to say that inequality between one society and another not merely creates conditions in which it is possible for the richer and more powerful one to intervene, but constitutes by its very nature dictatorial interference in the jurisdiction of the poorer and weaker society, then we are stating an absurdity.

An intervention always implies a decision to do something, when not doing it is also an option. If we say that it is the unequal relationship itself that is an intervention, and not the decision which this relationship helps to make possible, we not merely violate the ordinary meaning of the term, but also make it impossible to distinguish between those decisions of the richer and stronger party that are good or legitimate decisions, and those that are bad or illegitimate: rich and strong nations sometimes abstain from violating the rights of poor and weak neighbours, and sometimes provide aid and comfort to them. We also presuppose that equality of wealth and power between any two states or nations is a possible and desirable state of affairs, yet a moment's reflection should convince us that this is not the case. The United States and Mauritius may be equal in their rights as sovereign states, and their citizens equal in their rights as human beings, but there is no reason to think the two societies ever could or should be equal in wealth or power.

Moreover, although the vulnerability of Third World countries to Western intervention is something we should strive to correct, this is not a matter only or perhaps even chiefly of bringing about changes in the international system. It is a cardinal weakness of 'dependency theory' that in explaining the poverty and weakness of Third World countries so exclusively in terms of the impact of the international system upon them, it neglects the importance of domestic factors. The reason why 'dependency theory' hold such an irresistible attraction for Third World governments and peoples is that it provides a scapegoat for their own failures and inadequacies, just as the contrary theory, which places all responsibility on the Third World itself, provides a scapegoat for the governments and peoples of the West. It is now widely understood that domestic changes within Third World countries themselves are necessary for the reduction of poverty and social injustice within them, even if they are not sufficient. Such changes are no less necessary for the reduction of vulnerablity to outside intervention. If my argument above is correct, in this latter endeavour Third World countries have already had a considerable measure of success since 1945 compared with earlier periods, and this success has been founded upon processes of moral reawakening and political regeneration within their own societies.

Finally, even if we were to accept everything that has been said by 'dependency theorists' from Lenin and Kautsky to Frank and Galtung, or at least to acknowledge (as, indeed, we must do) that they have thrown a good deal of light on relations between the West and the Third World, we have still to insist that they have not presented a *general* account of intervention, any more than they have put forward a general account of world politics, of which intervention is one part.

Like Lenin's theory of imperialism, the neo-Leninist account of dominance and dependence in the contemporary world pertains only to the relations between the rich and the poor countries, the centre and the periphery. They have nothing to tell us, except in connection with the centre's dominance of the periphery, about relations between the rich and the rich, the strong and the strong, where the main issues of international relations have usually been thought to lie. Nor do they have anything to say—except, again, in the context of centre–periphery relations—about relations between the poor and the poor. They do not confront the classic problems of war and peace, conflict and coexistence among states and nations.

In the same way they have nothing to say to us about intervention as a general and recurrent phenomenon in world politics, but provide us only with an account of intervention by the Western capitalist powers in Asia, Africa, and Latin America. There can be no serious account of intervention in world politics today which does not also recognize Soviet intervention in the Third World and in eastern Europe also, and intervention by greater Asian, African, and Latin American states in the affairs of lesser ones. More fundamentally, the problem of intervention is bound up with the problem of the inequality of power among states, and this is a problem which has had to be faced in all periods of the history of international relations and in all places where international relations have been manifest.

NOTES

1 Ludwig Dehio, *Gleichgewicht oder Hegemonie* (Scherpe-Verlag, Krefeld, 1948).

2 John Gallagher and Ronald Robinson, 'The Imperialism of Free Trade', *Economic History Review*, vol. VI (1953), No. 1.

10

Collective Intervention

EVAN LUARD

The type of intervention with which this chapter is concerned
differs in many ways from the various forms of unilateral
intervention—intervention by one state in the affairs of
another—with which earlier contributions have dealt.

The first difference concerns its *legitimacy*. Unilateral
intervention has generally been seen—by countries other than
that which is intervening—as an undesirable activity. It is
manifestly self-interested: undertaken in the interests of the
power which undertakes the intervening. It may upset the
balance of power or influence among states. It is, generally
though not invariably, unwelcome to the government of the
country in which takes place. This can be measured by
normal use of language. No country announces that it is
'intervening ' in the affairs of another country: only that it is
providing 'assistance' to that country, 'restoring democracy', or
'preventing intervention by another power.' To the United
States the Soviet Union is 'intervening' in Afghanistan; in the
eyes of the Soviet Union it is assisting the present government
of Afghanistan by countering rebellion and intervention from
outside. To the Soviet Union, the United States is 'intervening' in El Salvador; in the eyes of the United States it is
providing assistance to the government of that country in
maintaining its authority and preventing intervention from
elsewhere. In other words, intervention is what other people
do, not what we do ourselves. This use of language clearly
demonstrates that intervention by a single state is an activity
that is not socially approved within the modern international
community.

Collective intervention, on the other hand, is by definition
intervention that has been authorized by some international
body having widespread legitimacy (we shall seek to refine
this definition later). Intervention by such an organization,
duly authorized, is widely seen as proper, even desirable. This

does not mean that a specific case of collective intervention may not be disapproved. So, for example, the Soviet Union disapproved of UN intervention to support South Korea during the Korean war; but this was mainly on the grounds that it had not been properly authorized (since the Soviet Union had not been present in the Security Council when the decisive resolution was passed) and therefore UN authority was being illegally arrogated. Some Western powers expressed doubts about the legitimacy of some aspects of UN intervention in the Congo; but this too was mainly on the grounds that the UN bodies or UN officials were exceeding their authority. In neither case was the *principle* of collective intervention contested. Collective intervention therefore, in general, possesses a legitimacy which is normally denied to unilateral intervention.

Secondly, collective intervention differs in its *purposes* from unilateral intervention. Unilateral intervention is undertaken by an individual state to promote its own special interests, whether political or strategic. It may be undertaken, as Stanley Hoffman suggested in an earlier chapter, to induce some other governnment to do what it would not have been likely to do by itself. It is anyway usually designed to bring about an end result—which may include the overturning of the other government concerned—more acceptable to the government which undertakes the intervening. It may sometimes be presented as promoting the interests of the country in which intervention takes place; but those interests are perceived by the country which intervenes.

Collective intervention is undertaken for collective purposes. Typically these might include such aims as stabilization, the restoration of the peace, the maintenance of the status quo, the exclusion of great power rivalries. These collective purposes do not normally include bringing about a change in the political balance in a particular state, which is perhaps the prime purpose of unilateral intervention. Those collective interests too are, of course, subjectively perceived: they are collective interests as understood by the majority within the organization which authorizes intervention. But such intervention will still be designed to promote common interests, even if it is only the common interests of the majority concerned; as against the interests of a single government, or a small number of governments, promoted by the intervention undertaken by individual powers.

Thirdly, the *methods* of collective intervention are also wholly different from those of unilateral intervention. For the methods are those available to the international organizations—whether world organizations or regional institutions—which undertake the intervention, and these are much more restricted than those available to national governments. Political interference, subversion, assistance to rebel forces, action to overthrow a government—these are not normally among the instruments available. Military intervention is rarely possible, and then only in very limited form. Economic sanctions are in principle available, but, being limited by the willingness of member states to apply them, are in practice hazardous and very rarely employed. Thus in general the means available to international bodies for intervening are far weaker than those available to national governments. If we were to think in terms of a contest between the type of intervention with which we are concerned in this chapter and those with which other writers have dealt in earlier chapters, we must thus be prepared for a gross imbalance of power. And it would therefore be rash to think that the answer to all the manifold problems of unilateral intervention described in earlier sections of this book can be found in the use of *international* intervention to deter or overcome the intervention of national governments.

Because collective intervention differs so radically from unilateral intervention, it could indeed be argued that the action that is undertaken by international bodies should not be classified under the term 'intervention' at all. Under a certain view of international politics there can be no such thing as 'intervention' by an international organization to which its members have accorded a certain degree of authority. In becoming members of the organization, individual states have at least implicitly recognized its authority. Intervention, therefore, in the sense of wrongful meddling or 'dictatorial interference', cannot be undertaken by an international organization. Even in taking measures which might reasonably be regarded as intervention if undertaken by national governments, such an organization is merely exercising its own lawful authority as it interprets it. 'Intervention' implies in some sense a breach of sovereignty; and such a breach of sovereignty cannot be committed, from this viewpoint, by an international organization, since a part of sovereignty has already been ceded to that organization.

It would even be possible to quote the terms of the UN Charter to justify this view. Under Article 2(7) of the Charter it is laid down that nothing that is contained in the Charter authorizes the UN to 'intervene' in matters which are essentially within the domestic jurisdiction of a member state. Many millions of words have been expended, both in debates within the UN itself and in discussions among international lawyers, about precisely what those words mean or imply. It is not necessary to enter into that lengthy and perhaps interminable debate here. It is sufficient to point out that the UN has in fact undertaken many actions which directly affect the domestic affairs of member countries. in seeking to end civil wars in Greece, Lebanon, the Congo, and elsewhere, in seeking to end apartheid in South Africa, in imposing sanctions against Rhodesia to bring it to end rebellion against Britain, and so on. In individual cases this has sometimes been contested as representing a breach of Article 2(7) of the Charter. For many years between the late forties and the early sixties colonial powers, for example, held that the UN had no authority for even discussing the affairs of dependent territories, since those affairs were, in the eyes of those countries, essentially within their domestic jurisdiction. Similarly the South African government has consistently claimed that actions of the United Nations which are designed to bring an end to the system of apartheid in South Africa likewise related to matters that are essentially within the domestic jurisdiction of South Africa. Such arguments have not, however, prevailed. And they have not prevailed on the grounds that the actions which the UN purported to undertake in each and all of those areas did not constitute 'intervention' for the purposes of Article 2(7): they could not be construed as representing the 'dictatorial interference' which international lawyers have traditionally been inclined to equate with intervention. On these grounds too, therefore, it could be claimed that whatever it is which the UN undertakes in relation to the affairs of individual countries—influence, pressure, exhortation, or collective action—it cannot, by definition, represent 'intervention'.

Whatever legal merits there might be in arguments along those lines, I do not intend to accept them for the purposes of this chapter. This is not only for the good practical reason that if I were to do so I would have to lay down my pen and write no further. It is for the much more compelling reason that such an interpretation seems to defy common sense. In normal language, few people can doubt that in certain cases international bodies, including the UN, do undertake something which we would normally regard as 'intervention'. Certainly they undertake intervention in the most precise sense of that word: that is, a coming-between. Where a UN peace-keeping force is sent to patrol a frontier or a cease-fire line, or to pacify a civil conflict, as in Cyprus or the Congo, the UN is, in this exact sense, 'intervening' between the combatants. In a more general sense UN actions, whether in civil conflicts or in international disputes, can represent an intervention, the interposition of new facts, a new reality, into the previously existing state of affairs: sometimes even within the previously existing *domestic* state of affairs of the country where the action takes place.

Having sought to establish therefore that collective intervention does indeed take place, and differs in important ways from the intervention undertaken by individual countries, let us go on to consider more exactly how the term should be defined. Almost every other writer in this series has attempted a definition of one kind or another of this elusive concept. It has been suggested that intervention can mean anything from the occupation of a country by armed force to doing nothing, from assistance to individuals or groups to assistance to governments. 'Collective intervention' too requires some measure of interpretation. And to undertake that we need to consider both halves of the term.

The world 'collective' could reasonably be used to apply to the participation of any group of countries in an act of intervention. Thus it could be suggested that intervention by Germany and the Soviet Union in Poland in 1939, or of US,

Australian, and other troops in Vietnam during the Vietnam war, or of Soviet, East German, and Cuban personnel in various countries of Africa in recent years, represented collective intervention. More plausibly, it could perhaps be applied to action by a collective organization, such as NATO or the Warsaw Pact. Though neither of these would be an unreasonable interpretation of the term (possibly multilateral or multinational might be more exact), they do not represent the usage which I will adopt here. For the purposes of this chapter (and I suspect of those who authorized the chapter) I intend to confine the use of the term to interventions by more generally representative organizations having a comprehensive, or near-comprehensive membership. In other words it will include actions by world-wide bodies, such as the UN and its agencies,; and it will include also actions by regional organizations such as the OAS (for example in initiating sanctions against Cuba) or the OAU (for example in dispatching a peace-keeping force to Chad).

The word 'intervention' presents greater difficulties. Other writers in this series have shown the difficulties of defining that term when applied to the interventions of single governments (where, under the widest interpretation, almost anything which one government does in relation to another could be construed as intervention). A government which dispatches a diplomatic note expressing concern about the nationalization of one of its concerns could scarcely be accused, under normal usage, of intervention. But if it accompanied the dispatch of the note with the dispatch of a flotilla of destroyers towards the coast of the offending state, then that term would not be altogether out of place.

A similar difficulty applies in relation to collective intervention. If the UN *discusses* the affairs of a particular state—say in a colony, on the system of apartheid in South Africa—this would not, on most interpretations, constitute intervention. Even if it were to pass a resolution on the subject, it is scarcely intervening in any meaningful sense. But if it passes a long succession of resolutions, if it brings pressure to bear by every available means, if it sets up a committee with the express purpose of mobilizing such pressures, then it can reasonably be said that a form of intervention takes place. For the purposes of this chapter, therefore, I shall not be concerned with cases where the UN or any other international body has merely *discussed* a particular circumstance, whether domestic or international, or even passed one or two isolated resolutions on the subject. I shall be concerned with cases where the UN has taken a series of steps which have been designed to influence events within a state.

There are many types of action taken by an international body which can affect the domestic position within a member state. They include actions undertaken by specialized agencies of the UN as well as by its political bodies. In some cases the acceptance of a degree of intervention by those organizations is a condition of membership. A member of the ICAO accepts an obligation to bring its navigation facilities up to a certain standard of efficiency and submits to a measure of inspection by the organization to see that this is attained. A member of the WHO undertakes certain obligations concerning the notification of infectious diseases, and again a measure of supervision to ensure that this is satisfactorily undertaken and the application of sanctions if it is not. A member of the IMF submits to a certain measure of surveillance by the organization of its exchange-rate policies. I doubt however whether any of these represent intervention of the kind with which we are here concerned: no nation is obliged to seek a loan from the IMF (and the conditions it demands are in no significant way different from those which would be demanded from any private banking organization from which credit was requested), nor to remain a member of ICAO and subject to its rules. These represent perhaps a form of collective influence, even of collective regulation. Collective intervention implies stronger forms of pressure—military, political, or economic—by the organization concerned. And it is with these that we shall be mainly concerned in this chapter.

Having defined the subject in this way, let us next consider the *reasons* why collective intervention has mainly been undertaken in recent years.

One reason why collective intervention has been called for is to counter or deter unilateral intervention. There are a number of fairly obvious reasons why unilateral intervention has become much more common in recent years; and especially in the years since 1945. The first and most obvious is the increase in power of the weapons now available. This means that the use of all-out war by a country to attain its aims, especially by superpowers, can involve risks which are totally incommensurate with the ends which are desired. How much easier, therefore, to undertake relatively limited action, often of an ambiguous kind, which may not provoke retaliation: to give assistance to friendly forces in another country, to help one side in a civil war, to engineer a *coup d'état?* Secondly, the instruments available for activities of this kind are much greater. In an age of ideological conflict, there are always sympathizers of almost every political persuasion who can be assisted; there are new methods of subversion; new methods of intelligence; new types of propaganda and political influence which can be employed. Thirdly, and most important of all, with the decline in distance has gone an outward extension of security zones. Until relatively recently, a country's security was held to depend mainly on its strength within its own frontiers, or only a limited way beyond. Today, the security of a country, especially of a superpower, is held to be affected by conditions throughout the area surrounding that power; and political developments which may affect the actions and attitudes of any government throughout that region may be seen as a threat. Thus it is that virtually every use of armed force by a major power since 1945 has been designed to ensure that politically congenial governments remained in power in areas immediately adjacent its borders which were believed to be vital to its security. So the Soviet Union has intervened successively in Hungary, Czechoslovakia, and Afghanistan (and some might say in Poland); the US has intervened in Guatemala in 1954, in Cuba in 1961, in the Dominican Republic in 1965, and (some would say) in El Salvador and Nicaragua today; China has intervened in Korea, Vietnam, and (many would say) in Cambodia today. This is a habit not confined to the great powers: smaller nations sometimes feel constrained to similar actions—for example Egypt and Saudi Arabia in Yemen, Tanzania in Uganda, Libya in Chad, Vietnam in Cambodia, and so on.

This increase in unilateral intervention leads to comparable demands for collective intervention to restrain it. The beliefs of the great powers about what is needed to maintain their security seem continually to expand. So the US could suggest ten years ago that the future of Vietnam was essential to US security; and certainly believes today that events in the Middle East are vital to that security. So the Soviet Union becomes involved (whether or not on security grounds) in various parts of Africa and the Arabian peninsula. Small powers see that these claims to global security interests can erode or destroy the political independence of weaker countries. In many cases, therefore, they invoke collective intervention as a means of resisting and containing such unilateral intervention by major powers. So in the Middle East UN forces have been created in part at least to prevent the area becoming excessively under the control of superpowers; so in the Congo a UN force was established in part at least to prevent that country becoming the arena for rival superpower activity; so in Cyprus a UN force was established to replace a purely British force and to preserve that island too from East–West conflict. The decline of distance, which increases the apprehensions of the superpowers, increases equally the apprehensions among small countries concerning the strength and influence of superpowers. International forces are sometimes seen as a means of countering that power and influence.

The superpowers themselves set limits to the use of this procedure. In their eyes international forces are a poor substitute for the methods which they have traditionally employed. It is not by chance, therefore, that UN forces have not been employed in East Europe, nor in Latin America (though there could well be demands for their use in El Salvador or Nicaragua). The aim of excluding excessive superpower influence is not seen, even by the smaller powers, as a realistic enterprise in these zones, so vital to the security of great powers. It is mainly in the relatively restricted no man's land between the superpowers, that is in Africa and the Middle East, that there has so far been recourse to collective intervention in the form of international peace-keeping forces.

Second, collective intervention has taken place—though only once—for the purposes for which it was mainly envisaged when the UN was established: for countering an attack by one state on the territory of another. Under Chapter VII of the

Charter, the UN was equipped with powers to raise forces of its own which would be used for that purpose when necessary. In fact those forces were never brought into existence; and this has sometimes been suggested as the reason why the UN has not more often intervened in defence of a country subject to attack. A more real reason is the lack of political will among members of the organization. The only occasion on which it was possible to reach agreement on a Security Council resolution calling on members to come to the assistance of a state under attack was in June 1950, when North Korean forces began to invade the territory of South Korea. Even in that case it was only possible because of the chance that the Soviet Union was absent from the Security Council at the time; and in practice the only countries to participate in the UN action were sixteen member states which would in all probability anyway have, for their own political reasons, agreed to give their support to South Korea in that situation. The type of collective intervention of which most was hoped, therefore, at the time when the UN was created has in fact been the kind that has been most uncommon and perhaps most unlikely to be repeated.

Third, collective intervention has been called for in a number of cases to pacify a civil conflict. This is, by contrast, a form of intervention which was probably scarcely anticipated at the time when the Charter was framed; and seemed to be almost prohibited by the terms of Article 2(7) quoted earlier. In practice the UN has become involved in a considerable number of civil wars. It has sent *peace-keeping forces* to the Congo, Cyprus, and Lebanon; as the OAU has to Chad. It has sent *observers* to Greece (1947-9), Lebanon (1958), and Yemen (1962-4). It has become involved in *humanitarian assistance* in a number of other cases of civil conflict. Such action, however, can normally occur only when the recognized government of the country concerned is willing to accede to it. And there are thus a large number of other civil conflicts—including for example, over the last few years in Cambodia, Ethiopia, El Salvador, and Guatemala—in which neither the UN nor any regional organization has become significantly involved despite widespread international concern.

Fourth, collective intervention has taken place in some

cases to ease the process of decolonization. Thus a UN force was sent, for example, to West Irian in 1962-3 for a transitional period to supervise the handover of authority from Dutch to Indonesian administrators. The UN force in the Congo ws originally sent in 1960 to supervise the withdrawal of Belgian forces which had been flown in to protect Belgian citizens in that country in the period immediately after independence. UN action against Rhodesia, including the imposition of economic sanctions, was under- taken to promote the decolonization of that country. Finally, it could be argued that the successive actions taken by the UN against South Africa, including the imposition of a mandatory arms embargo and the recommendation of other sanctions by the General Assembly, is designed to bring about a form of decolonization in South Africa—at least the abandonment of the system of separate development in that country.

Fifth, collective intervention has sometimes been called for to ease the process of withdrawal after a conflict has occurred. The first UN peace-keeping force, UNEF, established in Sinai after the Suez conflict of 1956, was dispatched in large part to supervise the withdrawal of the British, French, and Israeli forces and thus to provide them with some face-saving justifica- tion for withdrawal (since they were enabled to persuade them- selves that the UN force would protect the Suez Canal, even though that was no part of its function).[1] The force sent by the OAU to Chad in 1981–2 was designed in part to replace Libyan forces; and Libya was able to declare that its withdrawal was made possible by the decision to dispatch the force. In such cases the legitimacy of collective intervention, which is accepted even by those against whom the collective intervention primarily takes place, is used as a means of countering and ending unilateral intervention.

Sixth, collective intervention takes place in one or two cases simply to prevent chaos. Though the UN force in the Congo was intended in the first place to supervise the withdrawal of Belgian forces, it was retained in that country for four years after Belgian forces had withdrawn because it was generally believed that without its presence the country would have fallen into total disorder (that is to say into a still greater disorder than existed even with its presence). This is a cause of intervention which, more than most of the others, leads the UN into performing a role which is barely consistent with the sovereignty of the state in which intervention takes place. To prevent chaos the UN must be involved virtually in administering the country where it operates. This is what in fact occurred in the Congo: and the difficulties for the UN to which it gave rise—both political ones in New York and practical ones in the Congo itself—were such as to make it seem likely that the UN will seek to avoid such involvement again if it can possibly do so.

A final reason for collective intervention—and one which may become increasingly significant in the future—is the protection of human rights within particular states. At present this still represents intervention of a relatively modest and cautious kind. For years the UN Commission on Human Rights and its subcommission devoted themselves mainly to the drafting of general declarations, conventions, and covenants laying down general principles concerning the protection of human rights which were to be observed by member states, or at least by those countries which ratified them. But over the last decade or so, they have become increasingly involved (though normally at present only under confidential procedures) in considering the situation in individual countries and in issuing reports and recommendations. Since these recommendations normally become known, despite the confidential procedure, they come to have a significant impact on the countries whose affairs are judged, for example by being quoted widely by their opponents both within and outside their frontiers. The Secretary-General has himself on occasion appointed a representative to examine the standing of human rights in a particular country: as he decided to do, for example, in the case of Uganda during the Amin regime. Regional commissions of human rights have become more active and occasionally outspoken: the Inter-American Commission on Human Rights has issued hard-hitting reports about the situation in such countries as Chile, Uganda, and Argentina, and has undoubtedly had some influence on conditions in those countries. Though governments against which complaints are made can and do ignore recommendations of this kind, they none the less have some effect, above all on public opinion generally and perhaps thus ultimately on the actions of the governments concerned. Indeed the fact that the former head of the division within the UN concerned with human rights questions, who was partly responsible for extending and strengthening the UN's activities in this field, has now been removed from his post at the demand, it is widely believed, of certain Latin American governments, could be taken as an indication of the degree to which such activities have become effective and of concern to governments of that kind: no greater tribute could have been paid to the individual concerned. If a UN High Commissioner for Human Rights were to be established, as has been long proposed, with the function of examining human rights in particular countries, irrespective of the will of the governments of those countries, collective intervention for this purpose is likely to become more powerful and more persistent in the future than it has been in the past.

If these are the main reasons why collective intervention has occurred, what are the *forms* which that collective intervention has taken?

The most extreme form which collective intervention can take is the collective use of armed force. In its fullest sense—the use of armed forces which were expected to fight—this has occurred only once, in Korea. This might be said to represent the only occasion on which the principle of collective security has been applied, even approximately, in the way that has often been demanded. It was a case in which an international organization agreed (in however unusual circumstances) to call for the use of armed force by all the members of that organization (even though that call was a 'recommendation' rather than a mandatory 'decision') in defence of a country under attack. That it has not occurred more often need not surprise us. It results in part from the fact that, in a world as small as today's there is no incident in any part of the world, however remote, which is not seen to be of direct concern to one or other of the superpowers, which may therefore use its veto to prevent collective action of that kind. But it results even more from the difficulty which confronts any collective security system: that of inducing among individual members of the organization a sense that their interests are sufficiently threatened to require them to send their own armed forces, perhaps to the other side of the world, to defend some country of which they know little and care less. For both reasons it may be doubted whether this form of collective intervention is likely to occur frequently in the future.

It is clearly particularly difficult for international organizations to call for collective intervention in a case when war has already broken out. For in that event effective intervention will only occur if governments are willing to commit their forces to engage in armed conflict. For this reason collective intervention has much more frequently taken the form of the dispatch of forces which were not expected to be required to fight, but which might make it less likely that fighting would recur between two antagonists, whether contestants in a civil war (as in Cyprus or Lebanon) or the forces of different nations (as in Sinai or the Golan Heights). In practice the expectation that such forces would not be involved in fighting has not always been fulfilled. The UN force sent to the Congo was involved in substantial amounts of fighting, in different parts of the country and over a considerable period of time. One country withdrew its forces for that reason. The UN force at present in Lebanon has suffered a considerable number of casualties, some of them in direct conflict. It remains the case that governments are far more willing to commit their forces to operations of this kind than they would be to commit them to enforcement operations. The UN has not so far been prevented from undertaking such an operation because of the impossibility of finding governments willing to contribute troops. Peace-keeping forces of this kind can of course never be in a position to outweigh in power the national forces on either side which they are seeking to deter. The expectation is that the force will none the less have sufficient symbolic power to deter acts of force against it. In practice, it is believed, national governments will generally be unwilling to incur the wide-scale international opprobrium which would result from direct acts of force against a UN contingent of this kind.

The dispatch of peace-keeping forces represents, therefore, the most substantial type of intervention which international bodies can normally expect to be in a position to undertake. In other cases the UN has sent a force of observers to a troubled area. These may have the function of observing a cease-fire line and so, it is believed, of deterring action by either party across such a line: this has been to a large extent the role of UN observers in Kashmir, who have remained on the line between Indian and Pakistani forces for over twenty years. They may have the role of providing information which will enable political bodies of the UN to reach judgements on the infringements which do occur; this was the role of the substantial observer force sent to Greece in 1947-9, of the smaller force sent to Lebanon in 1958, and of those sent to observe the civil war in Yemen (in which Egyptian forces were heavily involved) in 1963-4. Here the volume of power available is minimal. In this sense it might perhaps be said scarcely to represent 'intervention' in the full sense of the word at all. Yet international bodies do in such cases demonstrate an active concern. And in this way a form of collective influence is exerted on international matters which cannot altogether be disregarded.

A type of collective measure which is, at least potentially, more significant is the use of collective economic sanctions. It has often been hoped that international organizations, in the absence of overriding military power, might none the less be able to exert their will through applying economic measures against countries which international governments sought to influence. Such measures have been used twice in international history: against Italy, in 1935-6 to induce her to withdraw from Ethiopian territory which she had occupied; and against Rhodesia in 1965-80, to induce the government of that country to abandon its unilateral declaration of independence, and return to colonial rule. Neither example provides striking evidence of the effectiveness of such measures. In the case of Italy sanctions were not even extended to some of the most vital commodities, such as oil, and were not applied by Italy's immediate neighbours and most important suppliers. In the case of Rhodesia, though sanctions undoubtedly weakened the Rhodesian economy and were possibly a marginal factor in encouraging its leaders towards accommodation, their effectiveness was minimized because of the existence of wholesale leakage through the Portuguese territories (until 1974) and South Africa. These examples show that economic sanctions are only likely to be an effecuive instrument of collective intervention if there is reasonable assurance that they will be universally applied, or at least universally applied by the main trading partners of the country against which sanctions are proposed. Since to have any mandatory force the sanctions must in any case be imposed by the Security Council, they can anyway only be applied against countries which it is in the interest of none of the permanent members of the Council to support. A lesser form of sanctions, an arms embargo, has been imposed by the Security Council against South Africa, which has no such backers; and the General Assembly has recommended the application of more general economic sanctions against South Africa, a recommendation which has been ignored by most of South Africa's chief trading partners. While therefore economic sanctions remain a weapon which is theoretically in the UN locker at all times, it is one which in practice it is not often possible to employ.

A more typical instrument of collective intervention is the use of systematic pressures against the country which the organization seeks to influence. Thus in seeking to bring about a change in the apartheid policies of South Africa, the United Nations has not only passed a long series of increasingly strongly worded resolutions, in a wide range of its constituent bodies and committees; it has deprived South Africa of membership of a number of its various constituent bodies; it has set up a special committee on apartheid which engages in continuous propaganda and other actions to promote the policies of the organization; it provides scholarships for victims of apartheid, that is, black Africans study abroad; it encourages and promotes the boycott of sporting links with South Africa, including the blacklisting of individual sportsmen; it supervises the embargo on the supply of arms to South Africa; and it promotes various other activities. The OAU, especially through its Liberation Committee, undertakes a number of similar activities, sometimes more far-reaching, including the encouragement of SWAPO operations in Namibia, and the recognition of banned black African organizations, such as the ANC in South Africa. The UN has undertaken somewhat less intensive campaigns against some other governments and systems: for example against the present government in Chile (though not, against other military regimes in Latin America, whose human rights record is certainly no better than that of Chile). The OAS has undertaken various diplomatic and economic sanctions against the government of Cuba. Finally, the UN Commission on Human Rights has brought to bear pressure of a much milder kind against a substantial number of governments (twenty or thirty so far) which it has found guilty of a consistent pattern of 'gross violations' of human rights. It is not easy to estimate how much influence any of these measures has had on the governments against which they have been directed. Not surprisingly, they have been denounced, resisted, and to a large extent ignored by those governments themselves. It is arguable that their most important effect is in the influence they have on *other* governments, and on the international environment generally: together they serve to establish the standards and criteria which are accepted within the international community as a whole. There are no governments today, for example, which seek to defend the system of apartheid in South Africa; and practically none which suggest that this is a purely domestic question with which no international organization ought to be concerned. And it is possible that the adjustments of the apartheid system which have been introduced over the last decade or so would not have come about, or would not have come about as fast, in the absence of the international pressures which have been exerted, and their impact on opinion in the countries whose goodwill is important to South Africa.

Activities of these various kinds can thus lead international bodies into close involvement in the domestic political affairs of a member state: an involvement which in principle such organizations are supposed to avoid. In acquiring a substantial responsibility for maintaining law and order in the Congo, the UN was obliged on occasion—even though it sought to avoid it—to make a choice between rival authorities, each claiming to represent the legitimate government of the country (and the action of UN officials in closing Léopoldville

airport in 1960 was decisive, it is sometimes said, in tipping
the balance against Lumumba and in favour of Mobutu). In
seeking to mediate between the leaders of the Greek-speaking
and Turkish-speaking communities in Cyprus, UN representatives had sometimes to make specific proposals about the
future constitution and balance of power in that country. In
its human rights activities the UN becomes automatically
involved in contentious domestic issues. Even in its decisions
about representation, the organization's members make
political judgements which can have repercussions on the
internal affairs of the country concerned. By declining to seat
representatives of Communist China for more than twenty
years after 1949, despite Communist control of the entire
Chinese mainland, by continuing to acknowledge the Pol Pot
regime in Cambodia as representative of that country for
years after it had ceased to control most of its territory, the
organization has taken a position on the domestic affairs of
particular countries. In decision of this kind collective actions
come closest in their purposes to unilateral intervention;
inevitably they have an impact on the domestic politics in a
particular country.

If these are the reasons why collective intervention has taken
place and the form which it has mainly taken, what have been
the final results of such intervention?

It is never easy to make such assessments. It is always
dangerous to conclude that because a particular state of affairs
succeeds a particular action that it must *result* from that action.
Even so it may be possible to venture a few tentative
conclusions.

Where the objective of collective intervention has been to
keep the peace, it is generally the case that the peace has in
fact been kept. In Sinai a period of continual conflict and
incident on the border between Egypt and Israel from 1950 to
1956 was succeeded in the following ten years by a period of
almost total peace after UNEF had taken over responsibility
for patrolling the frontier. Similarly after 1973, in the areas
where UN forces operated, in Sinai and on the Golan Heights,
peaceful conditions were maintained despite the bitterness of

the intervening conflict. In Cyprus, apart from one or two isolated incidents there has been little fighting between Greek-speaking and Turkish-speaking Cypriots during the eighteen years that the UN force has been operating there. In the Congo, though substantial fighting took place between different factions within that country during the period when UN forces were there, by the time they left the situation was probably rather more peaceful and stable than when they first arrived.

Again, in some cases collective intervention has been successful in maintaining or restoring the status quo. This is itself, it is true, a modest, and some would even say, a misconceived, objective. UN action, as has often been pointed out, has rarely been able to bring about those *adjustments* to the status quo which may sometimes be required if a long term resolution of conflict is to be secured. In Cyprus, though a substantial measure of peace between the two communities has been attained, no settlement of the long-standing political problems which divide them has been secured for all the intensive efforts which the UN has applied (for example, in sending a representative of the Secretary-General to mediate between the two sides, and in successive rounds of inter-communal talks under the authority of the UN Secretary-General). In the Congo, likewise, though the UN left that country in a somewhat more peaceful and better administered state than when it arrived, it did little to bring about a resolution of its domestic political conflicts (and indeed its departure was shortly followed by the coming to power of the politician against which its own activities had been most strenuously directed). In the Israeli–Arab dispute likewise, though the UN forces were able to maintain the peace of the area for lengthy periods, a settlement between Israel and Egypt was finally brought about, not through any of the intensive efforts at mediation which took place under UN auspices, but through the brokerage of one of the superpowers, altogether outside the framework of the organization. Though OAU forces in Chad were able to hold the ring for a period there, they were quite unable to bring about a settlement among the various factions which had for so long struggled for supremacy there (and war very soon returned).

In so far, however, as the maintenance of the status quo has been seen as a desirable aim of itself, collective intervention has in most cases secured it. In Cyprus the political and territorial situation remains now almost exactly as it was when UN forces first arrived there eighteen years ago. In Korea the final outcome of the UN operations was to leave the country in much the same divided state as it had been when they first arrived, with North Korean forces repelled to a line not unlike that from which they first emerged. In Lebanon the same complex balance of power between forces of the PLO to the north and of Haddad to the south, and between Syria and Israel beyond them, was maintained for years before the Israeli invasion of 1982.

In one or two of these cases the maintenance or restoration of the status quo has involved the restoration of the *territorial integrity* of the country concerned. As an organization of national states, the UN has inevitably been preoccupied with the protection of that integrity. Thus in the Congo it was firmly laid down that one of the purposes of collective intervention should be to defend and protect the integrity of the country; and UN forces were in fact instrumental in the reconquest of Katanga and its restoration to the central government's control. In Cyprus it has at all times been at least implicit in UN action that the final effect of a settlement should be to restore Cyprus as a single (though not necessarily unitary) national state. Even in Korea, where the country was already divided at the time when the UN first became involved, it was at least for a time the aim of UN intervention to restore the unity of the country (an aim which was used in part to justify the attempt to cross the 38th parallel in October 1950). This reflects an obvious common interest of the UN as a body representing sovereign states.

Collective intervention has been less successful in achieving one of the aims which many have had in mind when it had been set in motion: *keeping out the superpowers*, maintaining a particular country, or sometimes a much larger area, immune from great power intervention. In the Middle East, for example, despite long UN involvement, one of the superpowers at least remains dominant in a substantial part of the area (and indeed the main objective of those who demand a greater UN involvement today—for example through the convening of a new Geneva Conference—has been to counterbalance this through the influence of the other superpower). In the Congo, similarly, where the UN was perhaps more heavily involved than in any other country in its history, in time the country none the less came substantially under the influence of the US, and was eventually more closely identified with Western influence and interests than most of its neighbours in Africa. In Cyprus, though neither superpower is directly involved, Britian (and therefore NATO) continues to maintain bases in the country at the same time as UN forces operate there. Lebanon remains largely in the Western sphere of influence even though a UN force is heavily engaged there. In so far as the objective of any of these operations has been, therefore, to prevent the dominance of great powers in the area (and that has certainly not been the only objective), that aim has not been altogether accomplished.

This is only one illustration of the fact that, if collective intervention is seen as the means of deterring or reducing unilateral intervention, it has still a long way to go before it approaches the achievement of that aim. On the contrary, in the current state of renewed confrontation, the ambitions of the superpowers stretch ever further across the world. So now large areas of the Middle East, of Africa, of Asia, all begin to become part of the arena within which their confrontation is fought out. Neither is likely to be willing to rely on any form of collective intervention to protect its interests in such areas. At the most, collective intervention may occasionally be seen by one as a means of keeping out its antagonist from an area into which it might otherwise have penetrated (the OAS has sometimes been used by the US in this way). And for that very reason, in those cases, collective intervention is likely to be rejected by the opponent. As we saw at the beginning of this chapter, the instruments that are available to international organizations to undertake collective intervention are generally weak. This means that, especially where security interests are thought to be involved—and that today means in most of the world—collective intervention is unlikely to be welcomed by major powers (for this reason it is difficult to see the US permitting a role for the UN in Central America, for example).

Yet where it has been attempted, as in a number of the cases we have mentioned here, collective intervention has not been without success. It has maintained the peace; it has restored the status quo; it has protected territorial integrity; and it has in one or two cases even reduced the intensity of great-power conflict in an area where it might otherwise have been intense. Collective intervention will rarely be able to outface unilateral intervention. But the evidence suggests that, where attempted, it has a few successes to its credit. It may be that if the majority within international organizations were occasionally more bold in authorizing it, it could none the less sometimes have a more significant role to play.

For it is not only the superpowers which today become so frequently involved in intervention in areas outside their own borders. Most wars today take the form of civil conflicts, often with some degree of outside involvement. At this moment there are five areas of the world where conflicts of this kind are taking place on a substantial scale: Afghanistan, El Salvador, Morocco, Ethiopia, Cambodia. While in the first two cases it is superpowers that are involved (though in quite different degrees) in intervention from without, in the last three it is much lesser powers, with only marginal influence or support from superpower patrons. Whatever the difficulties of introducing collective intervention in areas where the superpowers are involved, these are far less where the intervening power is one of lesser stature. It may be that if the majority within international organizations were willing more frequently to take their courage in their own hands and propose it, collective intervention could more frequently play a role in reducing the intensity and frequency of unilateral action.

Until that time comes it seems unlikely that the type of intervention with which we have been concerned in this chapter will have a role to play that can in any way match, let alone overcome, the many kinds of intervention by national governments, more powerful, more manifold, and more dangerous, which have been described and analysed in the earlier chapters of this book.

NOTE

The international force set up to replace Israeli forces after their withdrawal from Sinai in 1982 is a similar example, though, since it is not a UN force, it does not strictly come within the definition we have established for this chapter.

II

Conclusion

HEDLEY BULL

I

The essays collected in this volume point to the conclusion
that intervention in the sense of coercive interference by
outside parties in the sphere of jurisdiction of a state is an
endemic or built-in feature of our present international
arrangements. In recent decades the interveners have to some
extent changed, in response to shifts in the distribution of
power: thus the Western great powers, the principal interveners of the last century, increasingly share the stage with the
Soviet Union and the stronger powers of the Third World.
Their modes of intervention have also changed: thus as the
legal and political obstacles to the older forms of intervention
have become more serious, forcible intervention has tended to
give place to non-forcible, direct to indirect, and open to
clandestine. We may argue as to whether this endemic
intervention is a new feature of the world political scene or the
continuation of an old one, and we may debate as to whether
it is to be deplored as a sign of the breakdown of an old
international order or welcomed as heralding the dawn of a
new one, but it is difficult to deny that it is a fact.

Stanley Hoffmann sees inherent contradictions between the
rule of non-intervention and the rule that states may maintain
their sovereignty by self-help, the rule that nations have the
right of self-determination; and the rule that governments
should conform to a principle of legitimacy. He argues that
neither international law nor international organization has
succeeded in controlling intervention; that the conditions
under which this might change show no sign of being realized;
and that the future of intervention is 'only too bright'.

Rosalyn Higgins's assessment is less bleak: she sees a role
for international law in attempting to reconcile the rule of the
sovereign equality of states with 'the reality of interdepend-

ence', especially by defining the international consensus as to where the distinction lies between intrusion which is acceptable and intrusion which is not. But here we have to notice the particular view of international law which she defends—that it is not a body of rules but a process of authoritative decision. While this view enables her to defend the role of international law in relation to intervention, it releases her from the necessity to defend the position that traditional international lawyers have maintained, that there is a strict body of rules about it.

Philip Windsor acknowledges that there are inhibitions on intervention by the superpowers, and holds that Soviet and United States interventionism are not symmetrical, inasmuch as there is no strict equivalent on the American side to the kind of intervention practised by the Soviet Union in eastern Europe. But he nevertheless argues that the ability of these two powers to affect activities within other states is so far-reaching that it may amount to 'structural intervention', a kind of intervention that is fundamental and permanent.

Dominique Moïsi's examination of the case of France emphasizes the unique features of its interventions in francophone Africa, and the limitations (possibly growing) which surround them, but he also brings out their considerable record of success. While the French interventions have had a formal legal basis in agreements entered into with former colonial territories, the validity of agreements conferring a right of intervention on a former colonial power would be disputed by much Third World opinion, which would also dispute Professor Moïsi's contention that French military actions during the colonial period were not interventionary in nature. Third World thinking is inclined retrospectively to label colonial pacification and policing operations as intervention, and also to insist that the rule of non-intervention includes economic coercion as well as military.

The new stimulus provided to interventionist thinking in the West by concern about access to resources is illustrated by Edward Luttwak's argument that a seizure of oilfields in the Middle East to restore oil production would be not only feasible and desirable but also morally and legally justifiable, in the event of an abrupt interruption of supplies, and on certain conditions. This argument, I believe, amounts to a claim that there is a right of forcible intervention not merely on grounds of self-defence, but on wider grounds of self-preservation, as was asserted by some international legal publicists in the last century. If it were to be acknowledged it might license a whole range of interventionary activity to obtain or secure resources held to be vital—not merely oil and not merely by the Western powers.

Michael Akehurst's essay brings out the challenge presented to the law restricting the use of force by the emerging law of human rights. While he urges the need for more effective international machinery to protect human rights, he argues strongly against the notion of a right of humanitarian intervention that entitles states unilaterally to intervene forcibly within other states in order to uphold the rights of their citizens, while also showing that in the post-1945 period such a right has been invoked by states on very few occasions, and then only to be generally condemned. Nevertheless, the growing moral conviction that human rights should have a place in relations among states has been deeply corrosive of the rule of non-intervention, which once drew strength from general acceptance of the principle that states alone had rights in international law.

Richard Falk's essay on the connection between intervention and national liberation shows the extent to which the United States and other Western countries have carried out interventions to suppress national liberation. We have also to remember that there are interventions to promote national liberation (as at the end of the eighteenth century by France on behalf of the American colonists against Britain, early in the nineteenth century by Britain on behalf of the Spanish colonists against Spain, or today by Cuba on behalf of black liberationists in Africa). The idea that international society recognizes a right to resort to force, not only on the part of states, but also on the part of nations that are not states, when they are seeking justly to liberate themselves, is one which has had a deep impact upon our present notions of lawful conduct in international relations, but there is little consensus about its meaning or import.

My own account of intervention in the Third World argues

that in the post-1945 period the peoples of Asia, Africa, and Latin America, who have been classic objects of intervention, have acquired a new capacity to resist the classic interveners, the Western powers, even though the old interveners have given place to new ones, the old forms of intervention to new forms, and lesser dependence on the international economy to greater. But it also argues that intervention is endemic in the inequality of power among states, and that this applies among Third World states themselves as much as between them and others.

Evan Luard, in his comprehensive survey of collective intervention, shows that intervention both by the UN and by regional bodies does indeed play a role in world affairs, but he also notes how far it is from reducing the role of unilateral intervention, how weak its instruments are in relation to those involved in the latter, and how impotent collective interveners are by comparison with the great powers.

On the one hand, great inequalities of power provide the conditions in which intervention is possible. On the other hand, the motives which give rise to it are widespread and insistent: economic motives such as the desire to acquire or to preserve access to resources; ideological motives such as the desire to promote social revolution or national liberation, or to oppose it; security motives such as concern to affect the global distribution of power; perhaps even humanitarian motives, such as concern to uphold human rights against tyrannical regimes. In a world political system as marked as is our own by interconnectedness and mutual sensitivity and vulnerability, such motives are scarcely to be avoided: our access to resources, the survival of our values and ways of living, our military security, and the human rights of others very often do depend on events within the jurisdiction of other states, which we can determine by intervening in them. Nor are such motives necessarily unworthy or discreditable.

II

Does this mean that it would be better to abandon the rule of non-intervention rather than maintain a pretence that states are bound by it? Normative structures may be conceived readily enough, in which this rule would have no place. In a world in which power and the authority to use it were concentrated in a central international authority, perhaps developing out of a strengthened United Nations, the rights of the authority to interfere coercively within the spheres of jurisdiction of the component political units might be unlimited. In a world in which power and authority were in the hands of regional international organizations, bodies such as the European Community, the Socialist Commonwealth of the Soviet Union and its allies, the Organization of African States, or the Association of South-East Asian Nations might similarly have unlimited powers of interference within particular regions, and the rule of non-intervention would have no place, except in relations among the various regional bodies. We may also imagine a world in which, in place of a rule of non-intervention, there was a rule confining rights of intervention to a limited number of great powers, each of which would be licensed to play the role of policeman in a particular part of the world: such a conception of international order, based on an understanding among a small number of regionally dominant great powers (the United States, the Soviet Union, Britain, China, India) briefly attracted the attention of planners of the post-war world during the Second World War, as an alternative to the United Nations system more in tune with the realities which then prevailed; in this kind of system the rule of non-intervention would play a role only in relations among the great powers.

In fact, however, the rule of non-intervention is essentially bound up with the rule that states are entitled to rights of independence or sovereignty. A state within whose sphere of jurisdiction there may be legitimate coercive interference by a world authority, a regional body, or a great power licensed to act as a policeman, is not independent or sovereign. Proposals to abandon the rule of non-intervention, along one or another of the lines sketched out above, are in effect proposals to abandon the principle that states have rights to independence, and to construct world order upon a quite different basis.

Whatever the merits of these and other visions of an alternative world order, it has to be recognized that none commands any significant degree of support among the .

political forces which prevail in the world today. There is an overwhelming consensus behind the principle that all states are entitled to rights of independence or sovereignty. It may well be that the system of sovereign states provides an imperfect or defective basis for world order from various points of view. The support that is given to the sovereignty of states is in many instances merely conditional or provisional, and the states which uphold it in principle sometimes depart from it in practice. But Western, Socialist bloc, and Third World states are united in treating it as the framework within which their relations with one another should be conducted. The support they extend to it is not merely lip-service, but is rooted in the interests they themselves perceive in maintaining their independence. Western countries may conduct experiments with the transcending of state sovereignty in their relations with one another, but even within the European Community, where these experiments have gone furthest, it remains the basis of their mutual relations. The Socialist countries may speak of a higher law of proletarian internationalism which qualifies their sovereign rights in relation to one another, but they do not proclaim that Socialist states do not have sovereign rights, and as they look outward they see these rights as a bulwark of their defences against capitalism. The peoples of the Third World, whose recent successes in transforming their position in the world have been achieved by the capture and exercise of state power, see the sovereign rights of their states as their most vital interests and as a bulwark of their defences against imperialism. The claims of states to sovereign rights, old claims that were first put forward on behalf of states that were princely or patrimonial, are today the claims of states which are popular or nation-states, or at least purport to be; the principle that the paramount rights are those of peoples, that international society is a society not merely of states but of nations, is one that complicates the rule of the sovereign rights of states, but it is also one that makes it ultimately more irresistible.

The consensus behind the rule that states have rights of sovereignty extends to its corollary, that they have the duty of non-intervention. The evidence that states today are willing to attach reservations and qualifications in principle to their adherence, as well as to violate it from time to time in practice, does not detract from this consensus, nor does it detract from the vital role which the rule plays in helping to define the basis of the present world order. Nor is it clear that the degree of disregard of the rule of non-intervention manifest in world politics at the present time is basically novel or unusual. The impression we have that the post-1945 period is one which is specially marked by interventionism is the result less, I suspect, of a greater incidence or severity of acts of coercive interference than in earlier periods, than it is of changes in our consciousness or perceptions: in a world in which intervention has come to be defined more broadly, condemned more loudly, resented more bitterly, reported more faithfully, we are more willing to recognize acts of intervention for what they are than we were in earlier phases in the history of international politics.

If there is a way forward now, it lies not in seeking to replace the rule of non-intervention with some other rule, but rather in considering how it should be modified and adapted to meet the particular circumstances and needs of the present time.

III

How, then, can the rule of non-intervention best be formulated so as to meet the requirements of world order in the closing decades of the twentieth century? First, we should insist that what is prohibited by the rule is action to interfere within the jurisdiction of a state; mere inequality of power between one state and another is not in itself an interference in the weaker state's affairs. It is necessary to make this point because in contemporary discussion of 'structural intervention' (whether of the Soviet Union in eastern Europe, of the United States in central America, of developed states in the affairs of less developed countries) there is a tendency to speak as if those who find themselves in a superior bargaining position in their dealings with other states or peoples are *ipso facto* involved in an infringement of the rules. Inequalities of power between states are, indeed, in many cases undesirable and remediable. They do sometimes give rise to illegitimate interference. Such interference is sometimes enduring and pervasive, and rightly called structural. The Third World thesis, that illegitimate intervention is sometimes economic in nature, is correct. But some inequality of power among states is inherent in the way the world is politically organized; moreover, given the enormous disparities in the populations of states, arithmetical equality of power (or wealth) among all states is morally undesirable. Most importantly, stronger powers are guilty of intervention in the affairs of weaker powers only when they engage in acts of illegal interference; if we are to say that they are as guilty of intervention when they forbear from engaging in these acts as when they engage in them, as guilty when they respect the rights of others as when they infringe them, the rule can serve no useful purpose.

Secondly, we should recognize that, in a world as marked as is our own by the political, social, economic, and strategic interconnectedness of its parts, the mutual involvement of peoples in one another's affairs is both inevitable and proper; the rule of non-intervention should be taken to prohibit forms of interference that may be agreed to infringe the sphere of jurisdiction of states, but should also permit those forms of mutual involvement which the material facts of our world appear to require, and its evolving norms to sanction. It is true that different societies at the present time take different views as to where the line should be drawn between what is infringement of a state's jurisdiction and what is not; whatever consensus may exist on this subject at any one time, moreover, is not static but is constantly evolving. It will be generally agreed that outside involvement in a state's sphere of jurisdiction, save in certain exceptional circumstances, will be illegal interference if it is dictatorial or coercive in nature. Third World states will include under this heading a wide range of economic pressures exerted upon them by outside parties, along with military pressures, and many states will also regard as illegal certain forms of interference that are not clearly dictatorial or coercive. The Western powers, in particular, whose capacity to involve themselves in the affairs of other peoples, whether politically, economically, or socially, is so much greater than that of many of the latter to involve themselves in the affairs of the Western countries, need to recognize that their own rather narrow definitions of illegal intervention are not universally shared. Nevertheless, developments in international law in recent decades, especially in the field of human rights, and the wider changes in moral attitudes to international relations of which these developments are an expression, provide a wide mandate for legitimate forms of outside involvement in what was previously considered the sphere of jurisdiction of states, which the rule of non-intervention should not be allowed to obstruct.

Thirdly, certain justifications for intervention which do in fact command support among some parties in the world today, and provide the motivation for dictatorial or coercive interference, are quite unacceptable because they are an affront to the existing consensus which, unless and until it changes radically, will remain hostile to them. One is the ideological justification, either of spreading communism or of extirpating it from the world; justifications of both kinds may be advanced, but not in terms of the requirements of international order, which is only possible today on the basis of coexistence of differrent social systems.

Another such justification is that which proceeds from the conviction that a particular nation or peoples is endowed by God or history with a role or mission that entitles it to impose its will on others for their own betterment. Such justifications of intervention, familiar in the history of European and other imperialism, play their part in shaping the policies of a number of states in the world today, not only the Soviet Union and the United States, but also certain lesser powers. My point is not that these justifications are always without foundation; indeed, it is not clear to me that they are always groundless, given that there are different levels of development, and I believe that it is wrong to mock them, as it is now fashionable to do. My point is that they have no prospect of being endorsed by the prevailing consensus; they fly in the face of the doctrine of the equal rights of peoples to independence, and can find no place in any agreed public doctrine of the rights of intervention.

We must also mention, as a justification of intervention which is entirely unacceptable, that which proceeds from a supposed right of states or nations to do whatever is necessary to preserve themselves. Such a right of self-preservation, held to be part of the 'natural rights' enjoyed by states irrespective of the society they formed with one another, was sometimes held to exist by positivist international legal publicists in the last century, and provides the intellectual basis of the so-called realist or Hobbesian approach to questions of international law and morality. It is, in effect, a denial of the rights of the society of states over its individual members, and is inherently destructive of international peace and security. The alleged right of consumers of natural resources, such as oil, in certain circumstances to seize what they need, adumbrated above by Edward Luttwak—a right which, once asserted by Western states in relation to oil may then be asserted by other states in relation to whatever resources they need—is tantamount to a return to such a doctrine of self-preservation.

Fourthly, it has to be recognized that today, as in the past, there are exceptions to the rule of non-intervention. We are not likely to have any strict body of legal rules about it that commands the consent of states, but only a loose set of moral and political precepts, principles, and precedents having varying claims to the status of law, such as Rosalyn Higgins and those who share her approach might regard as the international law of the subject, but others would consider to reflect the decay of international law. Opinion about these exceptions is divided and subject to change; in any given case the appropriate question will be about the degree of legitimacy it has, rather than whether it is legitimate or not. The answers given to this question will depend on the purpose or cause of the intervention; the means employed and whether they are proportionate to the end; and the auspices or authority under which the intervention takes place.

Now as in earlier periods the case for intervention will be strengthened if, other things being equal, it can be shown that it is at the request of the state in whose sphere of jurisdiction the intervention is taking place. An intervention that has the consent of the target state does not appear to infringe its jurisdiction in the same sense as one that is imposed on it. This argument, as we have noted, is still widely used as a justification: it is not the monopoly of the Western or any other group of states. A state's freedom to invite other states to undertake tasks within its sphere of jurisdiction is, indeed, an aspect of its sovereignty; and any suggestion that there could not be assistance of this kind by one state to another on the basis of consent would be generally regarded as intolerable. Whether we approve of this or not, the internationale of governments, which brings states of all descriptions together to maintain their leading position in the hierarchy of actors in world politics, will operate to preserve the future of this rule. We should note, however, that its appeal has been weakened by the progress of the idea that our judgements about intervention should take into account not only the right of a state to ask for assistance, but also the rights of citizens of that state, both collective and individual. Does the invitation to the intervening state have the support not only of the government but of the people? If there are circumstances of civil conflict, can the government be regarded as a legitimate one? How does assistance to it affect the human rights of its citizens?

Another old justification for intervention, that it is counter-intervention against a previous intervention by another state, is also bound to retain its appeal. To be in favour of counter-intervention is, after all, only to support the enforcement of the rule of non-intervention itself; it involves no appeal to principles or values that are in dispute among the main groups of states in the world today, and is employed on all sides: the United States at the present time uses it in central America, Cuba in Africa, the Soviet Union in Afghanistan, Israel in Lebanon. It seeks only to restore the conditions in which states can be independent and nations are free to determine themselves.

There is a need, however, for careful scrutiny of the counter-intervention argument. Is the alleged previous intervention a genuine one (John Foster Dulles, for example, once alleged that all communist party activity in the Americas was *ipso facto* Soviet intervention)? Is the counter-intervention proportionate to the initial intervention, or does it exceed it in scale (an objection sometimes made to United States counter-intervention in Vietnam)? Is the right to counter-intervene enjoyed by all states at large, or is it restricted to states directly affected by the initial intervention?

A basic justification for intervention will remain the

argument from considerations of defence or security. When intervention involves the use of force there will usually be an appeal to the right of self-defence: within the Western world at present there is a good deal of support for the concept of a right of self-defence which would sanction not only resistance to attacks of other states on one's territorial integrity and political independence but also forcible intervention to protect the lives (and on some views the property) of one's citizens in foreign states, to attack guerrilla bases in neighbouring countries which mount attacks on one's territory (and on some views to punish governments that play host to them and fail to control them), and (at a more subterranean level among a minority) to prevent the acquisition of nuclear weapons by a power that seems likely to menace one: the first of these kinds of intervention has been carried out by the United States, the second by South Africa, and all three by Israel. Third World countries, with the support of Socialist states, have condemned these forms of intervention, as it is natural for them to do, given that some of them have been the objects of it, and few yet have the capacity to carry out similar operations of their own: it might be wrong, however, to assume that intervention of this kind is destined to remain permanently the monopoly of the Western powers. Intervention in a broader sense—forcible and non-forcible, direct and indirect, open and clandestine—to maintain security by subverting unfriendly governments or sustaining friendly ones is widespread in the international community today, among all three of the main groups of states.

But given the present consensus about the use of force, the right of self-defence cannot be invoked (as it is so often invoked) to justify a wide-ranging right to interfere forcibly in the sphere of jurisdiction of other countries merely so as to advance the prospects of maintaining one's security; it may be sound security policy, for example, to check unfavourable changes in the distribution of power, but this can hardly be justified by appeal to generally accepted rules. The latter are likely to insist that the right to intervene exists only in response to an actual or threatened attack on one's territorial integrity or political independence (or on one's citizens, some would add); it can be exercised only if all other remedies are clearly exhausted; it must have a clear object; and it must, as in the case of counter-intervention, be proportionate to the end pursued.

As regards the future of the right of so-called humanitarian intervention, it is clear that the growing legal and moral recognition of human rights on a world-wide scale, the expression in the normative area of the growing interconnectedness of societies with one another, has as one of its consequences that many forms of involvement by one state or society in the affairs of another, which at one time would have been regarded as illegitimate interference, will be treated as justifiable. This does not mean, however, that states will be regarded as having a unilateral right of forcible intervention to uphold human rights within one another's territories. As Michael Akehurst shows, there is no present tendency for states to claim, or for the international community to recognize, any such right; it is very interesting that even in the recent cases in which interventions have been carried out which, it may be argued, have actually resulted in the advancement of human rights in the target states concerned, the intervening states did not claim this as the justification of their actions.

We should remember, also, how slender is the consensus that unites the governments of the world today in the matter of human rights. While they speak a common language on this subject, and while there is a wide area of agreement on what are sometimes called 'basic human rights', the emphasis of the Western countries on the rights of individual persons against the state contrasts on the one hand with a Soviet conception of rights as conditions brought about by the state, and with the emphasis placed on the other hand by Third World governments on collective rights. The reluctance evident in the international community even to experiment with the conception of a right of humanitarian intervention reflects not only an unwillingness to jeopardize the rules of sovereignty and non-intervention by conceding such a right to individual states, but also the lack of any agreed doctrine as to what human rights are.

The rule of non-intervention is also being affected by the doctrine of the Third World and Socialist countries that nations have the right to conduct just wars of liberation against colonial, racist, or alien domination. It is the implication of this doctrine not only that resistance to national liberation may constitute unjust intervention, but also that intervention to promote it may be justified. The Western countries have a number of objections to this view. Is not national liberation often taken to mean not simply establishment of the political independence of a nation, but political and social transformation by revolution? Is not the concept of just wars of national liberation applied opportunistically by the Soviet Union and others to whatever wars serve their political purposes? If nations have the right to liberate themselves, how are we to decide which groups purporting to be nations are rightly regarded as nations? How are we to judge the credentials of groups which purport to speak for these nations? Does not the right of national liberation entail the dismemberment of existing states? These objections raise serious issues, and the question of just wars of national liberation seems likely to remain a deeply devisive one for a long time to come. Nevertheless, it is necessary to recognize that the doctrine that nations have the right to liberate themselves has its historical roots in ideas of the rights of peoples and nations to determine themselves, of which the Western peoples themselves were original architects. The struggles for national liberation at work in Third World countries in the present era are part of a larger historical process of the transformation of an international society of princes or rulers into an international society of peoples, which is apparently irresistible, and which, despite present set-backs, in the long run may prove genuinely liberating for the peoples concerned. The Western countries, for all the legitimate doubts they have expressed, should not fail to take seriously the idea that intervention to suppress national liberation is unjust, and that intervention to secure the conditions in which it can take place may be legitimate.

Finally, intervention will be easier to justify if it is collective in nature. Such intervention—by the UN or by a regional international body itself, or by an individual state authorized to act by one of these bodies—already plays an important role, as Evan Luard's chapter shows; intervening states today will almost invariably seek some form of collective authorization, or at least *post facto* endorsement, of their policies. It is by no means clear that the trend which, considering this century as a whole, might be said to be discernible towards the collectivization of intervention, is bound to continue or to grow in force. What is clear is that the prospects for international order will be brighter if it does so.

The arguments we have considered for a right of intervention by an individual state would in every case be greatly strengthened if the intervener were a collective one, or at least acted as the agent of a collective body. The reasons why collective intervention is preferable to unilateral take us back to the contention of Christian Wolff that intervention is acceptable when it is carried out by the *civitas maxima*. Ultimately, we have a rule of non-intervention because unilateral intervention threatens the harmony and concord of the society of sovereign states. If, however, an intervention itself expresses the collective will of the society of states, it may be carried out without bringing that harmony and concord into jeopardy.

Index